The Little Book of BIG WORDS and how to use them

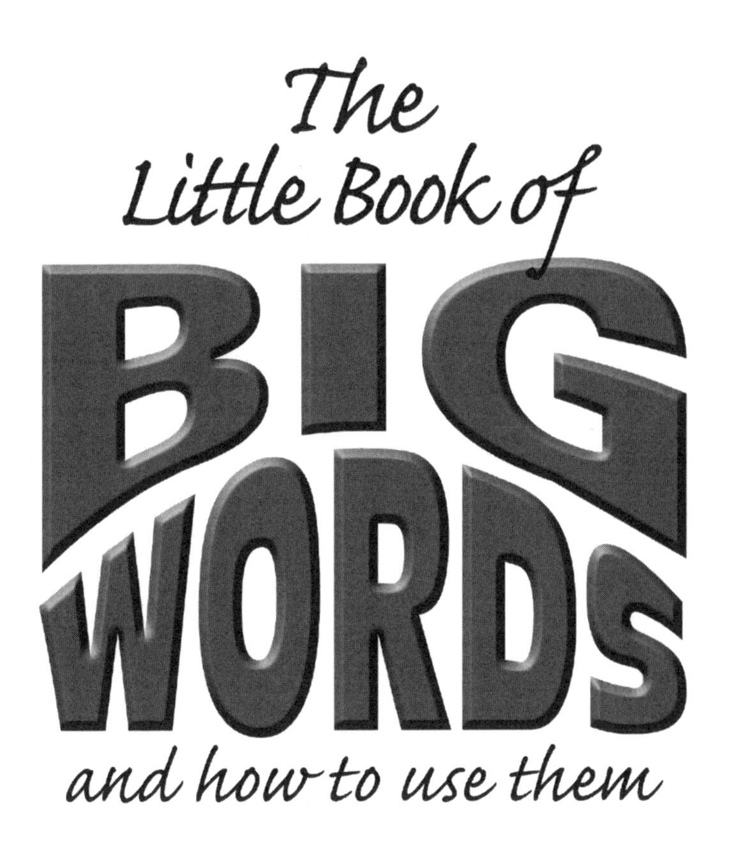

Andy Hughes

SPRING HILL

Published by Spring Hill

Spring Hill is an imprint of How To Books Ltd
Spring Hill House, Spring Hill Road
Begbroke, Oxford
OX5 1RX
Tel: (01865) 375794 Fax: (01865) 379162
info@howtobooks.co.uk
www.howtobooks.co.uk

British Library Cataloguing in Publication Data
A catalogue record for this book is available from the British Library

Cover Design by Mousemat Design Ltd
Produced for How To Books by Deer Park Productions
Designed and typeset by Mousemat Design Ltd
Printed and bound by Cromwell Press Ltd, Trowbridge, Wiltshire

ISBN10: 1-905862-03-2
ISBN13: 978-1-905862-03-0

Contents

About the author

Andy comes from a family of writers and teachers and so was raised in the 'world of words'. His book, *The Little Book of Big Words*, therefore, comes as no surprise to all who know him – the only surprise being that it has taken him so long to get around to writing it!

For the past fifteen years Andy has worked as a freelance news journalist and writer for radio stations such as Capital, Magic, BBC London, LBC, and BFBS Forces Radio, as well as ITN and IRN. During his career he has been responsible for writing and delivering news bulletins and features, as well as being on air covering such historical events as the deaths of the Princess of Wales and the Queen Mother, and various general elections. His writing skills have had to cover the tragic, the humorous and the downright silly side of all human nature.

As well as his radio career, Andy also lectures on radio presentation and has written for various weekly publications. It is only recently, however, that he decided to expand his writing career into the world of books, with *The Little Book of Big Words* being his first work and with several others on a variety of subjects also in preparation.

What is this book about?

First, this is *not* a dictionary. I wrote this book to try to improve your vocabulary. There will be words in here you know and some you have never heard before, but after reading this book, you will go on to use. There will be yet others you still won't use! However, you will know what they mean when someone tries to baffle you. Then there will be words that are of no interest to you whatsoever and that you think you have ignored and discarded, only to find that you have stored them in your subconscious for a later date!

The Little Book of Big Words is designed as a menu of longer words. You can choose those you like and start using them straightaway, with the help of the 'How to use this word' guides. But remember, there'll be words you think are simple, but to other people, will be new and exciting.

I'm always impressed by people who use simple words so everyone can understand them. But sometimes you need to use a big word if only to put down a patronising, intelligent person who is trying to intimidate you and to get one over on you. This book will arm you with some impressive words to use when you need to impress!

In some cases, where there is more than one meaning to a word, to keep it simple, I've just used the most common and well-known meaning. When I have referred to the Greek or Latin roots, I have tried to keep it simple, avoiding multiple meanings of words and tenses, but you will get the gist of the idea. As far as helping you with the pronunciation, I have given it to you, not in the correct and traditional way, but as a straightforward, 'street', phonetic version.

Andy Hughes

Acknowledgements

I would like to thank the following family and friends for their help in putting this book together: my very clever Dad, David Benson, Elizabeth, Helen and Rachel Benson, Stella and Philip Chryssikos, my agent Hilary George at Straight Line Management, Gwyn and Vicky Hughes, Kristian, Aaron, Ellis and Harry Hughes, Bridget Hughes (to be!), Emma Rafferty, Michael Rowan and Carol Venn, and last but not least my Mum for getting me off the sofa, inspiring me to do this book and then typing it all up! Without her you simply wouldn't be sat here reading it!

And, finally, I would like to dedicate this book to my Grandparents.

ABERRANT

This is a word meaning a deviation from the acceptable or the norm. It literally means to wander. It also means unusual, peculiar, irregular.

How to use this word

You could say that someone's extreme views may be seen as being socially *aberrant* to you or to others.

You could also say:

- 'Flamboyant artwork (or outrageous dress) may be seen as culturally *aberrant*.'
- 'The rules (or behaviour) of others that deviate from the acceptable or the norm could be considered *aberrant*.'

Alternatively, you could accuse someone of having *aberrant* views.

And finally . . .

So to recap, something that's a bit different is aberrant. When saying this word, it is pronounced **ab-ERR-unt**, making sure the emphasis is on the **ERR** part of the word.

ACRIMONIOUS

This word is used to describe a relationship between two parties that is riddled with hostility: a fight that's bitter, nasty, spiteful, harsh, cross, unfriendly, sour, ill-tempered, testy.

How to use this word

You could say, for example:

- 'It was an extremely *acrimonious* divorce.'
- 'I left my previous job under very *acrimonious* circumstances.'
- 'The negotiations continued in an *acrimonious* manner.'
- 'The two councillors running for office had an *acrimonious* relationship throughout the campaign.'

And finally . . .

When saying this word, the emphasis is on the third syllable, pronounced as **MOAN**. The pronunciation for the word is **acri-MOAN-ee-us**.

ACUMEN

This means keen insight, sharpness, wisdom, expertise, good judgement, perception, shrewdness, astuteness, ingenuity, discernment. It comes from the Latin word acuere ('sharpen').

How to use this word

You could say, for example:

- 'The millionaire showed great signs of business *acumen* from an early age, so I'm not surprised he's such a success.'
- 'She has considerable journalistic *acumen*, getting the story days ahead of her nearest rivals.'
- 'The MP showed great political *acumen* by making friends and allies on this matter.'

And finally . . .

When saying this word, it is pronounced **ACK-queue-mun**, taking care to emphasise the first syllable.

AD CAPTANDUM

This might be useful in a political discussion or educational exam – or even in the pub, for that matter! It's a Latin expression, still used today, meaning 'an argument that appeals to the mob, rather than to reason'. In other words, something that will keep the noisy, majority happy, but might not be the best course of action.

How to use this word

You could say:

- 'As an *ad captandum* argument, it doesn't actually help to resolve the disagreement (or issue).'

If a politician were attempting to appeal to and appease the mass majority by making unsubstantiated promises, you could say:

- 'That's an *ad captandum* statement and so I'm voting for someone else.'

And finally . . .

The longer version is 'ad captandum vulgus', meaning to win over the crowd.

ADULATION

This is another word for praise, worship, respect, admiration, idolisation. Other words to sum it up include respect, reverence and exaltation. It comes from the Latin word adulari ('flatter').

How to use this word

You could say:

- 'I always treated my boss with complete *adulation*, so her remarks about me being rude are nonsense.'
- 'I don't expect your staff to treat me with absolute *adulation*, but a bit of politeness and pleasantness would be nice.'
- 'The fans' *adulation* for Robbie Williams and his music is quite incredible and without limits.'

You can also thank someone for making his or her *adulatory* remarks.

And finally . . .

Your increased vocabulary (after reading this book) means your peers will have complete adulation for you. When saying this word, it is pronounced **ad-you-LAY-shun**, concentrating on the **LAY** part of the word.

ADVERSARY

This word refers to a competitor, challenger, opponent, rival, antagonist, foe or enemy. The context of how and what you're saying will determine the seriousness of the accusation. It comes from the Latin word adversarius ('opponent').

How to use this word

You could say:

- 'He saw her as his main *adversary* at work in the battle for promotion, as there was only one managerial position going.'
- 'Grahame was my main *adversary* for the job.'
- 'In the House of Commons the Prime Minister stood up to face his *adversary*, the Leader of the Opposition.'

And finally . . .

Adversary simply refers to opponents trying to achieve a similar goal, when there's a struggle and competition between them. It is pronounced **AD-vus-ary**, emphasising the **AD**.

AMBIDEXTROUS

This word refers to someone who can use either hand with equal skill and ability; a person who is neither predominantly left nor right handed. It comes from the Latin words ambi ('on both sides') and dexter ('right-handed').

How to use this word

You could say:

- 'I am *ambidextrous* (or you are *ambidextrous*).'
- 'He has lovely handwriting, perhaps either as a result of his *ambidexterity*, or maybe despite it!'
- 'Although naturally left-handed the man actually became *ambidextrous* after having his left arm in plaster for months!'

And finally . . .

In the age of qwerty keyboards, emailing, etc., are we not all now, in a way, ambidextrous? This word is pronounced **am-bid-DEX-trus**, emphasising the third syllable.

ANOMALY

An anomaly is something which deviates from the normal, expected or standard. It refers to an irregularity, inconsistency, oddity or peculiarity.

How to use this word

Perhaps you could say:

- 'Statistical *anomalies* can make it difficult to calculate whether society is getting richer or not.'
- 'I think the *anomaly* of having different waiters throughout the meal added to the slow speed of service and lack of understanding of our needs.'
- 'It was a bit of an *anomaly* seeing an empty motorway. I wish it was a public holiday every day!'

Mongolia (a land-locked nation) is represented at International Whaling Federation meetings. Some might say: 'What an *anomaly*!'

And finally . . .

I think the best way to understand this word is to use it in place of 'oddity', and then you can't go far wrong. It is pronounced **a-NOM-il-lee**, with the emphasis on the **NOM** part of the word.

APATHETIC

This describes someone who cannot be bothered, is indifferent or disinterested; someone who is impassive, with no enthusiasm, energy or desire for engagement with anything. It's a form of the word 'apathy'. You can show apathy towards a specific situation or behave apathetically.

How to use this word

You might say:

- (To a youngster who doesn't seem keen about tidying up) 'Don't be so *apathetic* and get on with it.'

- (To people around you who don't seem to care or to be eager to get on) 'Less *apathy* might help.'

Perhaps you might like to complain about, or even to, an *apathetic* sales assistant – after all, there are certainly plenty around!

And finally . . .

To sum up (if I can be bothered), someone who is apathetic has a whatever/whoever-may-care attitude towards things. When saying this word, it is pronounced **appa-THET-ick**, with the emphasis on **THET**.

ARACHIBUTYROPHOBIA

This word refers to a fear of getting peanut butter stuck to the roof of your mouth, which is, apparently, a phobia more common than previously thought. The fear stops the person concerned being able to think or speak properly, which in turn makes him or her feel sick, dizzy and breathless.

How to use this word

For example:

- I am, you are, he or she is an *arachibutyrophobe*.

- I am, you are, he or she is *arachibutyrophobic*.

- I have, you have, he or she has *arachibutyrophobia*.

Just notice the end of the word and how the last few letters change.

And finally . . .

This is one of those weird words that may come up in a pub quiz or a TV quiz show. If you get it right, please send me a percentage of the winnings!

ARCTOPHILE

This is a collector of teddy bears!

Below is a list of some other 'collector words'. They may be useful one day! Or perhaps you already are a collector of one of these but didn't realise your official title.

- *Cartophilist*: collector of cigarette cards.
- *Copoclephile*: collector of key rings.
- *Deltiologist*: collector of postcards.
- *Notaphilist*: collector of banknotes.
- *Numismatist*: collector of coins/medals.
- *Philatelist*: collector of stamps.
- *Phillumenist*: collector of matchboxes.
- *Porcelainist*: collector of porcelain.
- *Tegestologist*: collector of beer mats.

And finally . . .

Maybe there should be a word for 'a collector of big words'.

ARGUS

An unusual word used to describe someone who is ever watchful and alert, someone who keeps a constant lookout. It comes from the Greek mythological character Argos, who had a hundred eyes and who was eventually slain by Hermes.

How to use this word

For example, you could say:

- 'I've been *Argus*-eyed watching my children play all day in the park.'

Maybe you could complain about the watchful *Argus* eyes of someone making you feel uncomfortable.

And finally . . .

This word is always spelt with a capital letter – even mid-sentence – just as, for example, September or Capricorn would be. It is pronounced **ARG-gus**, with the emphasis on the first syllable.

ASSIDUOUS

Assiduous describes someone who carries out a task with great attention, diligence, persistence and concentration. This is someone who takes great care and effort over something; someone who is attentive, tireless, hard-working and persevering.

How to use this word

You could say:

- 'Elwyn has painted the front room this week. His *assiduousness* has paid off, because it's perfect.'
- 'The council has been *assiduous* in its fight against graffiti, but there's still a long way to go.'

You could also describe someone as an *assiduous* painter, singer, writer, etc.

And finally . . .

I have assiduously written every word of this book for you! The way to pronounce this word is **a-SID-jew-us**, with the emphasis on **SID**.

ASSIMILATE

This word means to absorb, digest, take in, learn, incorporate, take on board, integrate, blend in, adjust, conform. It can relate to something you're doing or to something that is happening. It comes from the Latin word similis ('like').

How to use this word

You could say:

- 'His mind was so distracted he could not *assimilate* all the information given to him by his bosses.'
- 'It's hard to *assimilate* so much detail when I'm revising for these exams.'
- 'The *assimilation* of the Irish into the USA over the generations has produced many Irish-derived names that now appear in American society.'

And finally . . .

We can also talk about the assimilation (mixing together, successfully absorbing) of all sorts of things. When saying this word, it is pronounced **a-SIMM-il-ate**, with the emphasis on **SIMM**.

AUDACIOUS

This means a bold or daring move, but a surprisingly cheeky or arrogant one as well. It also means risky, foolhardy, impudent, overconfident. It comes from the Latin word audax ('bold').

How to use this word

You could say:

- 'Well, if you hold out for a better deal in that meeting, then some would say it was a very *audacious* move.'
- 'I can't believe the *audacity* of that woman, asking for such a high price and refusing to move until she got it!'
- 'His plans are ambitious, shocking and *audacious*. I'll be surprised if he pulls them off.'
- 'I can't believe you have the *audacity* to criticise my work.'

And finally . . .

When saying this word, it is pronounced **or-DAY-shus**, with the emphasis on **DAY**.

AVUNCULAR

This word describes an 'uncle-like gesture', or the characteristic concern and kindness usually attributed to a kind-hearted uncle, in a positive, complimentary way. It derives from the Latin word avunculus ('maternal uncle').

How to use this word

You might want to say:

- 'David is very kind to Emily, the office junior, and, even though she is just a work colleague, he often makes *avuncular* gestures, such as giving her an Easter egg.'

- 'The school caretaker, George, has an *avuncular* disposition towards the children, often making jokes and buying sweets for them.'

- 'Edward is such an *avuncular* character when it comes to the children who visit his shop. He is always so kind to them.'

And finally . . .

When saying this word, the emphasis is on the **VUNC**, the second syllable, and it is pronounced **a-VUNC-queue-ler**.

BELLIGERENT

This word means hostile behaviour or a hostile attitude, a liking for conflict, a keenness to fight or quarrel. It derives from the Latin word belligerare ('wage war').

How to use this word

For example:

You can describe two nations as *belligerent* towards each other.

You can warn someone not to take such a *belligerent* tone with you.

You could say someone demonstrated such *belligerency* during a meeting.

You could also say:

- 'Some teenagers may appear to have a permanently *belligerent* attitude, particularly when confronted.'

And finally . . .

This word can be used correctly both at an impersonal level (two countries, two companies, etc.) and at a personal level (on a one-to-one basis). When spoken, the emphasis is on the second syllable, and the word as a whole is pronounced **bell-IJ-er-unt**.

BROBDINGNAGIAN

This refers to something that's gigantic, enormous, immense, colossal, extraordinarily large, huge, massive, etc. Right now I'm thinking of someone I know, or rather this person's bottom! Brobdingnagian has a bit more class, though!

How to use this word

You could say:

- 'Because of the interest, my overdraft has increased to such *Brobdingnagian* proportions I thought I would offer to increase my weekly repayments...'
- 'I was amazed to see the new sports hall at school. It's a *Brobdingnagian* building with enough space for the pupils to play a variety of sports all at the same time.'
- 'Mr Smith next door is over seven feet tall. His *Brobdingnagian* frame is an amazing sight, although I wouldn't like to fall out with him!'

And finally . . .

This word should start with a capital letter at all times. The reason for this is because its origin is in the name of the country, Brobdingnag – the land of giants visited by Gulliver in *Gulliver's Travels*, by Jonathan Swift (published in 1726). It is pronounced **brob-ding-NAG-ee-un**, with the emphasis on the **NAG** part of the word.

BUMPTIOUS

This word is used to describe someone who is self-assertive, offensively conceited in a presumptuous manner and perhaps overbearing. In other words, loud, big-headed and overly confident – 'cocky' in current street slang!

How to use this word

You could describe someone as being *bumptious*, or you could say someone has a *bumptious* manner.

Alternatively, you could describe how someone *bumptiously* put you in your place when you disagreed with him or her.

You could also say:

- 'In my opinion, his *bumptiousness* made him look silly.'

And finally . . .

When saying this word, the first syllable is pronounced the hardest: **BUM-shuss**.

CACOPHONY

This means a loud, hard or confused mixture of jarring sounds. It derives from the Greek words kakos ('bad') and phone ('sound'). Therefore, an unpleasantly harsh sound can be described as cacophonous.

How to use this word

For example, describing the horrendous noise you hear when you arrive at your weekly rehearsal for *The King and I*, you could say:

- 'As we entered the rehearsal studios we were met with a *cacophony* of instrumental sounds.'

Or you could say you were given a *cacophonous* welcome by the badly played instruments!

And finally . . .

The next time a bunch of your friends are singing in the pub, you could describe the rendition (or noise) as cacophonous. Mind you, try saying that after a few drinks! And if you can, then make sure you pronounce it correctly, which is **ca-COFF-any**, with the emphasis on the second syllable.

CAMPANOLOGY

This word refers to the study of bells or bell-ringing. Therefore, it will be a campanologist who will be ringing the church bells on a Sunday morning. The term also refers to a collector of bells of different shapes and sizes. It derives from the Latin word campana ('bell').

How to use this word

When the church bells wake you up in the morning, you could complain about the eagerness of the *campanologists* in the church tower.

Or you could say:

- 'I have no desire to hear the *campanologists* at work.'
- 'I'm going to ring the church bells every Sunday – my sisters are going to teach me all about *campanology*.'

And finally . . .

You'll be surprised how often you hear this word now! This is pronounced **camp-un-NOL-u-jee**, with the emphasis on the **NOL** part of the word.

CANTANKEROUS

This literally means one who is argumentative, bad-tempered and likes to quarrel. It is one of the simplest of the big words to use in modern-day speech and, because of the hard-sounding consonants in the word, it appears strong without being aggressive.

How to use this word

For example, we all know the man in the supermarket who is always moaning and trying to pick an argument with the poor checkout girl. We also know that he is always like that, because he is quite *cantankerous* by nature.

You could accuse someone of behaving *cantankerously* and say to them:

- 'You can be so *cantankerous* at times. Go away!'

And finally . . .

You pronounce this word **can-TANK-er-uss**, with the emphasis on the second syllable.

CAPRICIOUS

This refers to a sudden and foolish change of mind. It can be used to describe an unpredictable person – someone who is impulsive and erratic and prone to a sudden change of mind. It describes a person who makes a quick decision that is perhaps not the right one.

How to use this word

You could say:

- 'Tony is a *capricious* boss. He's dropped several projects that he was previously excited about, so we can't do them anymore.'
- 'Fred has gone back on his word and has *capriciously* applied for three more credit cards, without checking the interest rates and despite being massively in debt.'
- 'The *capriciousness* of my friend is unbelievable. She's just ordered a huge people carrier costing a fortune, despite being unable to drive.'

And finally . . .

I see this word as being similar to impromptu (see page 73) and unpredictable, although it describes an event that's slightly more serious. When saying this word, the **PRISH** part is dominant, so it's pronounced **ca-PRISH-us**, with the emphasis on the second syllable.

CATACLYSM

This is a sudden and violent upheaval, disaster, collapse or catastrophe; a great change, calamity or tragedy. It is often used in the context of something like an earthquake or flood.

How to use this word

You could say:

- 'This earthquake looks like it could be the biggest *cataclysm* of the twenty-first century.'
- 'The *cataclysm* that all but destroyed New Orleans has left thousands of people homeless.'
- 'My Dad reacted to the lack of cat food in the cupboard as a *cataclysmic* disaster and rushed out to the shops so that the cats wouldn't starve.'

And finally . . .

This is pronounced **KATT-A-kliz-um**, with the emphasis on the first two syllables: **KATT-A**. When using the word cataclysmic, the emphasis shifts to **KLIZ**: **katt-a-KLIZ-mick**.

CELERITY

The word celerity, rather appropriately, easily rolls off the tongue, and it is used to describe someone or something that moves quickly, with speed and swiftness. It comes from the Latin word celer ('swift').

How to use this word

You could say, for example:

- 'Now that Grandma's got her electric wheelchair she can move with much greater *celerity* to and from the post office.'
- 'Now that I've unbuckled the wheel on my bike and oiled it, it's moving with far greater *celerity*.'
- 'The birds move with such *celerity* as they fly through my garden that it's difficult to distinguish what they are or where they're going.'

And finally . . .

When saying this word, it is pronounced **se-LERR-ritty**, with the emphasis on the second syllable.

CHRONOLOGICAL

This word means sequential, consecutive, ordered, progressive, arranged in the order of the dates in which something happened. It comes from the Greek word khronos ('time').

How to use this word

You could say:

- 'The *chronological* order of these three Prime Ministers is Margaret Thatcher, John Major and Tony Blair.'

You could say you know the *chronology* of something; in other words, you simply know the order in which it happened.

You could also say that something has been *chronologically* presented to you.

And finally . . .

A real-life example of this word: the birthdays of my children, in chronological order, are 18 April, 26 May, 14 November and 27 December. See! I know the chronology and I told you chronologically.

CIRCUMVENT

This means to avoid, evade, get around, bypass, steer clear of, sidestep, dodge, get out of; find a way around a problem by being clever, often illegally.

How to use this word

You could say:

- 'Richard does a lot of his work cash-in-hand to *circumvent* some of those hefty tax bills.'
- 'Gary uses a lot of pirate software to *circumvent* those big price tags in the shops.'
- 'I'm trying to find a way to *circumvent* all these stupid rules.'
- 'Gwyn travels to Spain to buy alcohol to *circumvent* the high taxes in Britain.'

And finally . . .

It is pronounced **SUR-cum-vent**, with the emphasis on the **SUR** part.

COGITATE

To cogitate means to think deeply, to ponder about something, giving it much thought and consideration. You'll also hear people use the term 'cogitation'.

How to use this word

You could simply say:

- 'I have *cogitated* over the matter and have decided to . . .'
- 'I have been *cogitating* over the problem, and have decided it is not worth all the hassle.'
- 'Without need for further *cogitation* I have made my decision.'

You might also hear someone say:

- 'I would like you to *cogitate* about the series of errors which have occurred and attempt to reach a solution.'

And finally . . .

Just pretend it says 'thinking', and swap 'thinking' for 'cogitating' (i.e. to cogitate is to think). This verb is pronounced **COJ-it-ate**, with the emphasis on **COJ**.

COMMODIOUS

Commodious is a word used to refer to something or somewhere that is roomy or spacious. This word comes from the Latin commodus ('proper', 'fit').

How to use this word

You could use this word when describing your new flat, which, unlike your old one, is *commodious.*

You could grumble that your hotel room is not exactly *commodious.*

And finally . . .

Other things that can be described as commodious include a briefcase (which is deceptively spacious inside), a football stadium and even natural open spaces like a national park, or, of course, the classic example, the *Tardis*! This word is pronounced with a strong **MODE**: **cum-MODE-ee-us**.

CONCORDANT

This means in agreement, in harmony, unanimously at one, a state of treaty, showing unity and agreement together. It comes from the Latin word concordare ('harmonise', 'agree').

How to use this word

You could say:

- 'The two managers, formerly in dispute, worked together *concordantly* after resolving their differences.'
- 'It is essential that both mum and dad act *concordantly* in front of their teenage boys, for strength in unity will demonstrate a strict household.'
- 'The government is *concordant* on most matters in the run-up to the election in an attempt to show their strength as a political party.'

And finally . . .

When saying this word, it is pronounced **con-KOR-dunt**, with the emphasis on the second syllable.

CONFABULATION

This simply means to gossip, chatter, prattle, converse, natter, talk. It refers to general discussions rather than malicious gossip. It comes from the Latin word fabula ('story', 'tale'), which interestingly is also the root of the word 'fable'.

How to use this word

You could say:

- 'There was some *confabulation* about where we should meet and what the dress code should be.'
- 'They gathered to *confabulate*. The matter must be resolved today.'
- 'The bosses have been *confabulating* all day about whether the pay rise should be 1 per cent or 2 per cent.'

And finally . . .

You have probably heard the abbreviated version of this word many, many times. For example: 'We had a quick confab about when the event should take place.' This word has the emphasis on the second syllable, and it is therefore pronounced **con-FAB-you-lay-shun**. If you use confab, the emphasis shifts to the first syllable: **CON-fab**.

CONJECTURE

This word means reaching a conclusion with incomplete evidence; making a statement or judgement by guesswork. If you form an opinion without all the relevant information, then you're drawing a conclusion and reaching that opinion by conjecture.

How to use this word

If someone says to you: 'I believe that person in court, on television, is guilty, as charged.' You could respond:

- 'Well, without the full facts of the case, your speculations and assumptions are pure *conjecture*.'

On a TV programme a politician may have said the next election is on 10 May. But you could say:

- 'In the absence of an official announcement by the PM it is merely *conjecture*.'

You could also say:

- 'Speculation about the Loch Ness monster is always based on *conjecture*.'

And finally . . .

There is a strong emphasis on the second syllable, so you pronounce it **con-JECK-ture**.

CONVIVIAL

This means lively, warm, friendly, sociable, welcoming, fond of good company. It comes from the Latin word vivere ('live').

How to use this word

After a party you could say:

- 'Thank you so much for having me. You're a very *convivial* host.'

You can describe a function or home as *convivial* because of its welcoming, friendly and warm atmosphere.

Perhaps you could complain about a bar or hotel by saying:

- 'I was most disappointed by the lack of *conviviality* on the premises.'

And finally . . .

Try to learn this word because it is a very positive and therefore could get you lots of Brownie points for being nice! When saying this word, the emphasis is on the second syllable: **con-VIV-ee-ul**.

CORNUCOPIA

This describes a large amount, abundance, plenty or excess of something. It comes from the Latin words cornus ('horn') and copia ('abundant supply').

How to use this word

You could say:

- 'There was a *cornucopia* of shoes for sale at the market. I bought several pairs.'
- 'There's a *cornucopia* of golf books at the library. They must have at least a hundred different ones, and I just couldn't choose which one to take out.'
- 'There was a veritable *cornucopia* of pastries waiting for us when we went down for breakfast in the hotel, but I was disappointed there was no hot food.'

And finally . . .

There's a cornucopia of fascinating words in this book. Try to use a few of them and remember the others so you are able to understand them when some clever clogs tries to baffle you! When saying this word, it is pronounced **corner-COPE-ear**, emphasising the **COPE** part of the word.

DENIGRATE

This means to make critical or negative comments about something or someone, in a way so serious that it may damage a reputation; remarks used in a defamatory context, literally meaning to blacken a reputation. It comes from the Latin word niger ('black').

How to use this word

You could say that bad remarks passed about your character could be described, in your defence, as *denigratory*.

Remember, *denigratory* comments are usually unfair and unjust criticism. You shouldn't *denigrate* others just because they have different political views from yourself.

And finally . . .

This word is pronounced **DEN-i-grate**, with the emphasis on the **DEN** part of the word.

DIFFIDENT

This word is used to describe someone who is lacking in self-confidence, is rather timid and a little shy, or someone who is restrained and reserved in behaviour. It comes from the Latin word diffidere ('mistrust').

How to use this word

You could describe someone as *diffidently* entering the room by saying:

- 'Ellis shyly poked his head around the door before *diffidently* making an entrance.'

Or

- 'A *diffident* Ellis entered the room, but not before popping his head around the door.'

And finally . . .

There are several alternatives to this word, such as reticent, unobtrusive and hesitant. It's not an offensive or derogatory word if used in the right manner and context. It is pronounced **DIFF-id-unt**, with the emphasis on the first syllable.

DISCOMBOBULATING

This is a word which means to confuse the issue or matter, or to make things generally confusing.

How to use this word

You could tell someone his or her complex argument is *discombobulating* by saying:

- 'I think you've taken on board too many sides to this argument and have *discombobulated* the original issue.'

Maybe, if someone adds another angle or idea to a discussion, you could say:

- 'No, that just *discombobulates* the matter even more.'

If I give you any more examples, I will just *discombobulate* the explanation or make it *discombobulating*.

And finally . . .

It is a rare word, but good to know. It is pronounced **diss-com-BOB-ulating**, with the emphasis on the third syllable.

DISQUIET

This word means unrest, uneasiness, concern, anxiety, worry. It also signals fear, alarm, distress, fretfulness and agitation.

How to use this word

You could say:

- 'There's a certain amount of *disquiet* at work as we've heard there may be some redundancies.'
- 'The *disquieting* situation between Jeremy and Robert looks set to go on. They're still not talking to each other.'
- 'The teacher's constant absence and intermittent appearances for lectures are causing *disquiet*.'
- 'There's *disquiet* within the political party as they wait to see whether or not its leader is going to step down.'

And finally . . .

This is pronounced **dis-KWHY-ut**, with the emphasis on the **KWHY** part of the word.

DRAGGLE

OK, time for a fun word. I'd never heard of this one prior to my research, but I'll be using it from now on! It sounds like such fun that, really, it should be the name of a cartoon character, but it actually means to make something wet, dirty and lifeless by dragging it along.

How to use this word

This is a simple one, really. You could say:

- 'I *draggled* the sheet along the garden path and so had to wash it again.'
- 'Who *draggled* the shirt through the mud? Now I need to clean it again.'
- 'Don't *draggle* your scarf out of the car door.'

And finally . . .

This seems to be a rare word as not many people I asked had heard of it. It is pronounced as read.

DULLARD

A beautifully insulting word for you to use here – if you must! It refers to someone who is a dunce (ironically, a dunce won't know what the word means!). To sum up, it describes someone who is a dull person, dope, simpleton or ignoramus.

How to use this word

You could say:

- 'You are such a *dullard*.'
- 'He (or she) is a *dullard*.'

And finally . . .

How easy is that? But if you are scratching your head at the explanation, then you know what you are, don't you? I have met many dullards in my life, and if only I had known about this word then! This word is pronounced exactly as read, with a slight emphasis on the **DULL** part.

DUPLICITY

This means fraud, trickery, double-dealing, dishonesty, dissimilation, fraudulence, deceit. It's the act of deliberate deception in speech, attitude or behaviour. It comes from the Latin word duplex ('double', 'two-fold').

How to use this word

You could tell someone you were taken in by his or her *duplicity* or even that you were disappointed by his or her deliberate *duplicity*.

You could also accuse someone of being *duplicitous*.
For example, you could tell a *duplicitous* shopkeeper that his prices are too high.

And finally . . .

When saying this word, the emphasis is on the second syllable, which is actually pronounced **PLISS**. The whole word is pronounced **jew-PLISS-itty**.

ECLECTIC

This word refers to a collection of something from different beliefs, assorted methods and diverse sources. In other words, a lot of different things from everywhere.

How to use this word

You might say:

- 'There was an *eclectic* mix of people at the party.'
- 'There was an *eclectic* mix of restaurants in the town where we went on holiday: Thai, Italian and French.'
- 'This CD has an *eclectic* mix of music genres from all over the world.'
- 'When I saw Alan's house, I realised he had an *eclectic* taste in furniture. There was a mix of old and new and an array of different styles.'

And finally . . .

It is pronounced **eh-KLECK-tic**, concentrating on the **KLECK** part of the word.

ELEPHANTINE

What a great word! It's literally used to describe something as a big as an elephant, but in a more gracious way – almost! It means mammoth, massive, colossal, enormous, gigantic, gargantuan, huge. Something elephantine is oversized and unwieldy, and it is normally used negatively to describe somebody's (or something's) size.

How to use this word

You could say:

- 'I've put on so much weight over Christmas that I feel *elephantine*.'
- 'The tiny pile of rubbish at the end of the garden keeps growing and has now become simply *elephantine*.'
- 'Does my bum look *elephantine* in this?'

And finally . . .

This can be quite a nasty word used in the wrong context and with vicious intent. It paints a very clear picture about what you are talking about! It is pronounced **ELLA-fun-tine**, with a slight emphasis on the **ELLA** part.

ELUCIDATE

This is a great word to be armed with if you're making a complaint, for it means to explain, clarify, reveal, expose, make clear, shed light on, spell out, illustrate. It comes from the Latin word lucidus ('bright', 'clear').

How to use this word

You could say, for example:

- 'I was not happy with the service I received at your shop from the moment I stepped through the front doors. Please allow me to *elucidate* on the catalogue of catastrophes.'

- 'I really don't understand. Can you *elucidate* further?'

And finally . . .

I hope I elucidated the word clearly enough for you. If not, allow me to elucidate further. All the TV newsreaders have been elucidating on the local elections and who's running for what. Clear now? Remember to pronounce it **il-LOOSE-id-ate**, emphasising the **LOOSE** part.

EMPIRICAL

This word means knowledge of something based on experiment, experience and observation. It also means something that is pragmatic and practical, rather than just being based on theory. It comes from the Greek word empeiria ('experience').

How to use this word

You could say:

- 'I have heard Jack is a lazy worker, but my *empirical* view, as a colleague by his side, is that he's hard-working, meticulous, keen and considerate – plus, he gets results.'
- 'This project is backed up by *empirical* data collected over several weeks, so please give it your careful consideration.'
- '*Empirical* studies show that 20 per cent of people prefer listening to the radio rather than watching TV.'

And finally . . .

It is pronounced **em-PIR-ic-cul**. The emphasis here is on the second syllable.

ENSCONCED

This refers to someone comfortably established in a place – be it in a chair or in the position of President. It gives the impression that the person concerned is ready to stay a long while. The word can also refer to the act of hiding something away for secrecy.

How to use this word

You could say:

- 'I'm *ensconced* on the sofa, surrounded by chocolate, alcohol, cushions and the remote control, with my feet up. Read my lips: "I'm not moving."'
- 'The boss is firmly *ensconced* in her position of power, despite being useless at her job and a nasty woman. There seems no way of getting rid of her.'
- 'I am *ensconced* in your arms. This would make a nice romantic photo, wouldn't it?'

And finally . . .

It is pronounced **en-SCONSED**, heavy on the second syllable.

ENTENTE

This word means a friendly but informal agreement between two countries. It can often be heard in international political documentaries or discussions. The 'Entente Cordiale', for example, was an agreement between France and Britain to stop arguing over matters in other countries. It was signed in 1904 and still stands today. It's not a word you can use much, but it's good to be able to understand it when media reporters talk about efforts to create some kind of entente.

How to use this word

Next time you're discussing the troubles in the Middle East, you could say:

- 'It's a shame that the Israelis and Palestinians don't create an *entente* over their borders to settle the issue once and for all.'

You could also say that a quarrelling couple have reached an *entente* following their dispute over who gets the money, property and children.

And finally . . .

When saying this word, it is pronounced **on-TONT**, with the emphasis on the second syllable.

EPICURE

This word refers to someone who has a refined or sensitive taste, usually in his or her choice of food and wine. It's quite a positive word and is generally used on a complimentary basis, rather than critically.

How to use this word

You could say, for example:

- 'We have selected the finest food and wine for someone with such a distinct *epicure*.'
- 'We went shopping before you arrived – your *epicurism* for expensive chocolate is well known.'

When tasting an unusual or expensive wine, you could say:

- 'Mmm, nice, but you've got to have the right *epicure* for that particular vine.'

And finally . . .

This is pronounced **EPPY-cure**, harder on the first part.

EQUANIMITY

A word used to describe a calmness of the mind. It comes from the Latin words aequus ('even') and animus ('mind').

How to use this word

You could say that you dealt with a difficult situation with a sense of *equanimity*. In other words, you didn't get flustered or emotional!

You could also say that, after having looked at both sides of the argument with *equanimity*, you have still decided to stick with your original plan.

Alternatively, someone might ask you:

- 'Do you look upon the troubles with anger, regret or mere *equanimity*?'

In other words, do you get bothered or do you look at it in a calm, sensible way?

And finally . . .

This word is pronounced **eckwa-NIM-itty**, with the emphasis on the third part, **NIM**.

EQUILIBRIUM

This means a state of balance; a state where influences are cancelled out by others to create a balanced, steady and stable situation. It can also be used to describe a calm and controlled emotional state. Or, in modern parlance, 'chilled out'.

How to use this word

You could say:

- 'There's a certain state of *equilibrium* at home, as the arguing has stopped and it's now all quiet.'
- 'I'm not going to mention tomorrow's problems as everyone is quiet and it may upset the *equilibrium*.'
- 'There seems to be a state of *equilibrium* between the two rowing neighbours right now, as recently they haven't argued at all.'

And finally . . .

Just think of equilibrium as a posh word for chilled-out-ness and you won't go far wrong! By the way, just so you know, there are scientific uses for this word too, like thermodynamic equilibrium, quasi-static equilibrium and punctuated equilibrium. And if you're still awake, in the world of finance, economic equilibrium describes a balance of supply and demand. You might hear that one on the TV news. It is pronounced **ee-kwa-LIB-rium**, with the emphasis on the third syllable.

ETYMOLOGY

This word means the study of the derivation of words. Be careful not to confuse it with entomology, which is the scientific study of small bugs and insects. If you do that, it would be a malapropism (see page 95 to explain that!). Etymology comes from the Greek word etumos ('true').

How to use this word

You could say, for example:

- '*Etymologically*, a butterfly was once called a flutterby before metathesis (see page 105) changed it.'
- 'Those clever individuals who have studied Latin and Ancient Greek are streets ahead when understanding the *etymology* of the words we use every day.'
- 'I studied the *etymology* of words for my English degree and found it very interesting.'

And finally . . .

It is pronounced **etty-MOL-ijee**, harder on the second part.

EULOGISE

This word means to glorify, acclaim, praise, wax lyrical, extol highly. It also means to sing the praises of, rave about, exalt, command. In other words, in street speak, 'to really dig something and big it up'.

How to use this word

You could say:

- 'The DJs on all the radio stations have *eulogised* about Elton John's new single. They really dig it!'
- 'The crowds *eulogised* the Man United players as they came on to the pitch for the Cup Final.'
- 'Val came out with this great *eulogy* about her old English teacher, saying how she taught her so many big words.'

And finally . . .

A eulogy, by the way, is an article, speech or poem that praises someone who has died. A eulogy can also be written for someone who's stopped working after a long time. When saying this word, the emphasis is on the first syllable, and the whole word is pronounced **YOU-lu-gize**.

EUPHEMISM

This is an alternative and subtle expression used to represent something else. In other words, it is when we use one word to replace another . . . while everyone knows what we really mean all along!

How to use this word

Someone may ask you:

- 'Are you really asking me in for a coffee, or is that a *euphemism*?'

In this case, coffee may well be a *euphemism* for sex!

On the other hand, a *euphemism* can be used to replace an offensive or un-politically correct term. For example, 'senior citizen' is a *euphemism* for an 'old person', while 'pre-owned' can be a *euphemism* for an old, second-hand item.

If you 'suggest' to someone something along the lines of 'Your carpet has seen better days', that's a *euphemism*. What you really mean is: 'Your carpet is old and dirty!'

And finally . . .

All these are correct, but the first example of coffee/sex is how it's mostly used these days. This example uses an alternative, less offensive word than sex, but everyone will know what is meant by the speaker's tone of voice and the context in which the sentence was spoken. When saying this word, it is pronounced **YOU-fam-iz-um**, with the emphasis on the first syllable.

EUPHORIA

Here's a nice cheerful word meaning an exaggerated, great feeling of joy, elation, happiness. It comes from the Greek word euphoros ('borne well', 'healthy').

How to use this word

You could say:

- 'When I heard about my promotion, I was in a state of *euphoria*.'
- 'I have been in a *euphoric* state all day after winning at bingo last night.'
- 'I have been *euphorically* clearing out my desk on my last day of this terrible job.'
- 'There was a feeling of *euphoria* at college on the last day of the exams. The students *euphorically* ran to the pub after the last bell.'

And finally . . .

This word is pronounced **you-FOR-rea**, harder on the **FOR** part.

EUROPHILE

An explanation of this word may come in handy for those political discussions, and its meaning is very straightforward. A Europhile is an admirer of Europe or the European Union. I would describe the late Edward Heath (who wanted a United States of Europe) as a Europhile. A Europhile wants closer ties between Britain and the rest of the European Union.

How to use this word

You could say:

- 'Harold was a *Europhile* and so decided to learn four European languages during and after his university course.'
- 'During our business negotiations, Annabelle, as a committed *Europhile*, decided most of the contracts should go to countries in Europe.'
- 'During the elections the *Europhiles* were campaigning to drop the pound in favour of the euro in order to create closer ties with Europe.'

And finally . . .

When saying this word, it is pronounced **YOUR-a-file**, with the emphasis on the first syllable.

EXTEMPORANEOUS

This word describes delivering a speech, presentation, sermon, off the cuff, without notes and without practice. It means to do something or perform an act in an impromptu way – that is, without preparation or practice. It comes from the Latin words ex tempore ('at the time') – an expression used widely in legal circles.

How to use this word

You could say:

- 'Tom delivered an *extemporaneous* speech at the company dinner last night, and made some funny points about the way we work.'
- 'It was an *extemporaneous* performance I witnessed, but witty and charming, none the less.'

And finally . . .

This is not really used as a negative word. 'An extemporaneous but perfect guitar recital' just means the guitarist didn't need to practise for hours on end, and he surprised us with his performance. It is pronounced **ex-TEMP-por-ain-eus**, with the emphasis on the second syllable.

EXUBERANT

This refers to someone who is lively, vivacious, elated, effervescent, high-spirited, energetic, lively, enthusiastic, excited; it can also mean lavish and flamboyant.

How to use this word

You could say:

- 'He's a young and *exuberant* little boy who can't get enough of life. He's always charging around the house and garden.'
- 'The fans *exuberantly* greeted the actor at the stage door.'
- 'I love Reece's *exuberance* after he's had his afternoon nap: he seems to come to life all over again.'
- 'I really appreciated the waitresses' *exuberance*. It made the whole exciting place come to life.'

And finally . . .

When you say this, the emphasis is in the **ZOO** part: **ex-ZOO-bi-runt**.

FALLACIOUS

This describes something that is totally wrong, fictitious, false, misleading, incorrect; something that is mythical or untrue.

How to use this word

You could say:

- 'The claims that have been made against me are totally *fallacious* and should be treated with contempt.'
- 'I object to the *fallacious* remarks that have been made against me. They must be withdrawn at once and an apology issued.'
- 'Your advert *fallaciously* claims that your product comes with batteries and makes blackcurrant juice turn green. These claims are unacceptable and I demand a full refund.'

And finally . . .

In my opinion, or experience, I think the best and most accurate way to use this word would be to say: 'It's a complete fallacy that women are better cooks than men!' Fallacy is pronounced **FAL-as-see**, and fallacious is pronounced **fal-LAY-shuss**.

FATUOUS

A nice and simple alternative expression when referring to someone who stupidly or foolishly thinks that . . . The spirit of this word means, in my stupid and innocent naivety, I thought you'd have fixed it, resolved it, done it by now. It means inane, stupid – as in making daft or silly remarks, which can then be described as fatuous. It comes from the Latin word fatuus ('foolish').

How to use this word

You could say:

- 'I have continued in my *fatuous* belief that your company should have fixed this problem by now, but it remains…'
- 'It was my *fatuous* hope that you would have sent me a refund by now, but this has not happened.'
- 'Perhaps, with great *fatuity*, I thought that this problem would have been resolved by now.'

And finally . . .

It is pronounced **FACH-you-us**.

FAUX PAS

This term means an embarrassing blunder that breaks a social convention of some description. It is a French term, literally meaning 'false step'.

How to use this word

You could use it in this way:

- 'The drunken best man's *faux pas* of the day was the moment he gave the speech at the wedding reception and talked in detail to all the guests about the bride's ex-lovers, including the bride's parents.'

One *faux pas* that was reported globally was when the Prime Minister of Australia put his arm around the Queen. This was described as an embarrassing *faux pas* as the world watched and cringed. The reason is that no one is allowed to touch royalty.

And finally . . .

You pronounce this word **foe-PAR**, with the emphasis on the second syllable.

GARRULOUS

This refers to someone who talks too much about something of no particular importance. It can be used to refer to someone who jabbers or natters, and who is talkative, wordy and voluble. It comes from the Latin word garrulus ('chattering', 'talkative').

How to use this word

You could say:

- 'Gail is most *garrulous*, talking often from dawn till dusk!'
- 'With her *garrulous* tongue, Bethan entertained us for hours.'
- 'Geraint entertained us *garrulously* all night, but I haven't the faintest idea what he was talking about!'
- 'Oh, and Geraint? His *garrulousness* is one of his funny and sweet qualities.'

And finally . . .

It is pronounced **GARRUL-us**, with the emphasis on the first part of the word, getting quieter as the word goes on.

GERRYMANDER

Here's a word you'll do better to understand rather than use, I think. It means to manipulate, withdraw or change political districts or boundaries to the advantage of a certain political party. The word derives from nineteenth-century US politics, although the practice of gerrymandering went on for many years before that. In 1812, Governor Elbridge Gerry of Massachusetts gave his own party an advantage over its opponents. They called him a 'salamander' (a lizard-like animal), and others cried 'make that a Gerrymander' – and the word stuck. When you hear politicians talking on TV today about boundary changes, there's usually someone shouting 'this is Gerrymandering'.

And finally . . .

It is pronounced as read.

GORMANDISE

I love this word. It refers to devouring, guzzling or stuffing. It's a lovely way to describe someone who gorges, crams, bolts, eats greedily or devours his or her food gluttonously. Three things spring up from my childhood memories here: food, being told off and having to slow down – this word paints such a picture!

How to use this word

You could say, or shout if you must!

- 'Harry, don't *gormandise* your food.'

I dare say there'll be a look of bewilderment on little Harry's face, but it will have the desired effect when he stops to try to work out what you mean!

You can call someone a *gormandiser* (equivalent to a greedy bolter of food).

You can also accuse someone of *gormandising*. For example: 'Don't *gormandise* that pie – nobody is going to steal it!'

And finally . . .

Pronounced **GOR-mun-dize**, this is a colourful, succinct, image-provoking word. Notice I have used an 's' instead of a 'z' as in the American version, which is **GORMAN-DIZE**.

GRAVITAS

This describes something with weight, seriousness and substance to it. It comes from a Latin word that is also spelt gravitas ('seriousness').

How to use this word

You could say:

- 'The speech lacked any real *gravitas*, just lightly touching on a few topics. We needed more things covered in greater depth.'
- 'There was real *gravitas* to the message he sent. We knew he meant business by the nature of it.'

And finally . . .

Just think of gravitas as meaning a strong message with real depth and power, and you won't go far wrong. It is pronounced as read. The emphasis is on the first part of the word when saying it: **GRAV-it-ass.**

GREGARIOUS

This word is used to describe someone who is sociable, very friendly and enjoys the companionship of others. In other words, a friendly little soul! It comes from the Latin word grex ('flock').

How to use this word

For example:

- 'My girlfriend was very *gregarious* at the party. She went round and spoke to everyone. She is so good at socialising.'
- 'I made a point of *gregariously* going round and meeting all the new neighbours, and of saying "hello" to them.'
- 'I was impressed with my teenage son's *gregariousness*. He made a point of chatting to all my friends when they came around.'

Yeah, as if that would happen! It would more likely be:

- 'My teenage son shows no sign of being *gregarious* when we have company. He just hides in his room.'

And finally . . .

It is pronounced **grig-GARE-rius**, with the **GARE** part the strongest.

HALITOSIS

An interesting word to describe a simple medical condition that you and I would simply call 'bad breath'. Not to be confused with myxomatosis – a disease commonly found in rabbits! That would be a malapropism (see page 95). It's not a word we use very much, but I've heard it being bandied about as an insult once or twice, so make sure you understand what it means. There's nothing worse than hearing an insult and not understanding it – you might say 'thank you' by mistake. So in this look-perfect, weigh-perfect, bleached-white-teeth society of ours, I felt it's a word worth knowing.

And finally . . .

It also crops up in the lyrics of the song 'My Friend', a number in Willy Russell's musical, *Blood Brothers*. See, you even need to know 'Big' words to enjoy a musical these days! It is pronounced **hally-TOE-sis**. The hard sound here is on the **TOE** part.

HIPPOPOTOMONSTROS-ESQUIPPEDALIOPHOBIA

Ironically, this word refers to someone who has a phobia about long words. Use this and you'll confuse everyone! Learn how to spell it and you'll be a genius!

How to use this word

The best time to use this word has to be when some Smart Alec tries to baffle you with a long word. You could just say to him or her:

- 'I'm sorry, but I suffer from *hippopotomonstrosesquippedaliophobia.*'

He or she will then know how it feels!

And finally . . .

How do you pronounce this word? With great difficulty! Nobody seems to know. But at least you now recognise the meaning and can include it in an angry letter to someone.

HIRSUTE

This is a great word to describe a man who is hairy. It's a slightly affectionate or humorous way of talking about someone's hairiness without being offensive.

How to use this word

If you know a man who's growing a beard (or maybe hasn't shaved for a few days), you could say how much you admire his new *hirsute* image, or ask him if his *hirsute* look is permanent. You could even say you like his *hirsuteness*.

You could also say:

- 'It's not fair that beards are banned at work considering there are a number of *hirsute* managers.'
- 'Our bosses have a hatred of *hirsuteness* in the workplace, despite there being a number of bearded managers.'

And finally . . .

It is pronounced **her-SUIT**, with the emphasis on **SUIT**.

HURRY-SCURRY

This refers to something done in a rushed and hurried way, resulting in a confused mess.

How to use this word

Imagine that, one day, when you were in a rush, you put all your bank statements in order, only to find that, at a later date, some of the pages are actually out of order. Your excuse could be that you did it in a bit of a *hurry-scurry*.

Perhaps one day when you brought in the washing, quickly during an unexpected downpour, it all got mixed up. Why? Because you were in a bit of a *hurry-scurry*, of course!

And finally . . .

It is pronounced as read.

HYPOTHETICAL

This is a frequently used word that means to assume for the sake of an argument, 'just to pretend for a moment that'...

How to use this word

I am going to be *hypothetical* now and give examples of things that unfortunately are not going to happen.

Let's just say, *hypothetically* speaking, that I was a millionaire. I might buy you a new car.

And speaking *hypothetically*, if I were Prime Minister I would do away with tax for anyone whose initials are AH! (Andy Hughes!)

And finally . . .

This word is pronounced **hyper-THET-ical**, with the harder sound on the **THET** part of the word.

IDIOSYNCRASY

A word used to describe someone's funny little ways; an action or a thought associated with a certain person. It comes from the Greek word idios ('private').

How to use this word

Take the simple task of making tea. If I insist on putting the milk in my tea before the sugar, I could tell you that it is:

- 'Just one of my little *idiosyncrasies*.'

Or I could say:

- 'Putting milk in my tea first is just one of my little *idiosyncratic* ways.'

Alternatively, you could say:

- 'My mum always makes sure the bathroom towels are laid out in perfect straight lines. It's just one of her little *idiosyncrasies*. If they're messy, she has to line them up in her *idiosyncratic* way.'

And finally . . .

When saying this word, it is pronounced **idd-ius-SINK-rassy**.

IGNOMINIOUS

This is simply a great substitute for the words humiliating, embarrassing, shameful, disgraceful or discreditable.

How to use this word

You could use this in a letter of complaint to a company, describing your *ignominious* experience in their shop, restaurant, etc.

You could talk about your *ignominious* list of previous lovers or debts, for example.

You might also want to say:

- 'The soldiers *ignominiously* retreated from battle after their defeat.'

You could perhaps ask someone who is in disagreement with you:

- 'Can't you see the *ignominious* look on my face after what you have just said?'

And finally . . .

This word is pronounced **igna-MIN-ee-us**.

IMPROMPTU

This refers to something that's spontaneous, unplanned, unrehearsed, offhand, spur-of-the-moment, unprepared, off-the-cuff, ad lib, unpremeditated. It comes from the Latin phrase in promptu ('readiness').

How to use this word

You could say, for example:

- 'Uncle Ernie had rehearsed his wedding speech but, having lost it on the way to his nephew's reception, he had to give an *impromptu* speech when he stood up.'

- 'At David's retirement party, his line manager stood up and gave us an *impromptu* rendition of Will Young's song, "Leave Right Now". Not really the best choice, but then he was drunk!'

- 'At work, Helen handed out lots of chocolates as we'd been slaving away. That was such a kind, *impromptu* gesture.'

And finally . . .

I wasn't planning to put this word in the book – it was just an impromptu decision. It is pronounced **im-PROM-chew**, with the emphasis on **PROM**.

INANIMATE

This word is used to describe something that has no life and that cannot move. In other words, an object that's motionless, without life, dead, inert (without the power to move). The horse, for example, is animate (it is an animal), but the cart is inanimate (it is an object).

How to use this word

You could say:

- 'When I made an office in my bedroom I put a few lamps and books around the room. It's amazing how a number of *inanimate* objects can make such a difference.'
- 'Why does my sofa keep moving backwards away from the TV? It's so annoying. How can an *inanimate* object irritate me so much?'
- 'When I'm trying to get to sleep at night I can sometimes hear noises in the house, despite nobody being there – its just a house full of *inanimate* objects.'

And finally . . .

Think of the horse and cart, where the horse is alive and the cart is the inanimate object. Interestingly, when Walt Disney made inanimate pictures move, they became animated and so the process was described as animation. When saying this word, it is pronounced **in-AN-ee-mut**, with the emphasis on the second syllable.

INCLEMENT

This word refers to stormy, drastic, harsh, unmerciful or severe weather, and it comes from the Latin words in ('not') and clemens ('gentle').

How to use this word

You could use this word by simply referring to the consistently *inclement* weather during a long and hard winter. Or you could say you're fed up with the *inclement* weather tiring you out.

You could also say:

- 'The weather is unusually *inclement* for the time of year.'

In other words, it's awful weather considering it's September!

You could, of course, always use it in an excuse to impress, or to confuse, people and say something like:

- 'Because of the *inclemency* of the weather, I won't be able to make it to the WI jam-making exhibition tonight – it's 145 metres up an icy hill.'

And finally . . .

When saying this word, it is pronounced **in-CLEM-unt**, with the emphasis on the **CLEM**.

INCONGRUOUS

This word means conflicting, contradictory, unsuitable, incompatible, out of place, inconsistent.

How to use this word

You could say:

- 'It looks rather *incongruous* having that modern Ikea chair sitting in the middle of my antique-styled, oak-beamed study.'
- 'It seems *incongruous* to me to have a male journalist working on a women's magazine.'
- 'The *incongruity* of staying in a five-star hotel and having chips on the menu every day is unacceptable.'

And finally . . .

Just see the word as replacing 'the weird', 'the unsuitable', and it will work. When saying this word, make a harder sound on the **KONG** part of it: **in-KONG-gru-uss**.

INDEFATIGABLE

This word means someone who just won't get tired, weary, exhausted or fatigued. It comes from the Latin word fatigare ('fatigue').

How to use this word

You could say:

- 'I must praise my estate agent's *indefatigable* hunt for a new house within my set price range. His hard work has finally paid off.'
- 'My son has been *indefatigably* studying for his exams over the last two weeks.'
- 'I must praise the dancers' *indefatigability* in the high-energy, non-stop musical I saw last night in the West End. They were brilliant.'

You might commend a long-standing colleague at work for his or her hard work and *indefatigability*.

And finally . . .

It is pronounced **in-de-FATT-ig-abul**, harder on the **FATT**.

INEXORABLE

This means inflexible, immovable, adamant, unrelenting; it also means not to be moved by or persuaded otherwise. It's a great word to arm yourself with in an argument or when writing a letter of complaint.

How to use this word

You could say, for example:

- 'Having had my new washing machine repaired twice since I bought it, I now must insist on a full refund. I am *inexorable* on this matter and look forward to your immediate and productive response.'
- 'I will not tolerate your lateness, young man. Your curfew is 10 o'clock and I am *inexorable* on that. It's not 10.30!'
- 'I have *inexorably* stated that the new carpet should be bottle green and not lime green, so please bring the right one.'

And finally . . .

It is pronounced **in-EX-erabul**, with the emphasis on the **EX**.

INFINITESIMAL

This refers to something that is tiny, minuscule, insignificant, microscopic, minute, imperceptible, negligible. It comes from the Latin word infinitus ('endless').

How to use this word

You can describe something as *infinitesimally* small:

- 'The chance of me doing x, y or z for you today, I'm afraid, is *infinitesimal*.'
- 'Thankfully, the amount of rain we had on holiday was *infinitesimal*.'
- 'The boss has only *infinitesimally* increased our salary, yet we are still expected to be grateful!'

In a letter of complaint you might want to write:

- 'There was an *infinitesimal* serving of vegetables at dinner, and we were not happy.'

And finally . . .

Another word spoken as read, but do remember to put the emphasis on the third syllable: **in-fin-TES-im-ul**.

INNOCUOUS

This word means harmless, or unlikely to cause harm or offence. It comes from the Latin word nocere ('injure').

How to use this word

Let's take the old lady next door who keeps moaning about your untidy lawn. You might describe her nagging each morning as fairly *innocuous* because, after all, she is just trying to keep the village tidy: there are no threats, no nastiness and no wicked intent. You might describe her as *innocuously* reminding you every morning to keep your lawns tidy.

You could also say:

- 'Chris is such a quiet little soul, *innocuous* in every sense of the word, and wouldn't harm a fly.'

And finally . . .

You pronounce this word **in-OCK-you-uss**, harder on the **OCK** part.

INSTANTANEOUS

This means something that happens immediately, straightaway, on the spot, suddenly. It also means done instantly, with a speedy reaction and as quick as a flash.

How to use this word

You could say, for example:

- 'After the show, there was a standing ovation: the whole audience *instantaneously* got up .'

Or

- 'The standing ovation was *instantaneous*.'

You might also say:

- 'When the Health Secretary announced a cut in nursing levels, there was an *instantaneous* response from the unions, who called for a strike ballot.'

- 'When our mum shouts "DINNER!" the entire family *instantaneously* runs from all directions to assemble in the dining room.'

And finally . . .

It is pronounced **in-stan-TANE-knee-us**, with the emphasis on the third syllable.

INSURMOUNTABLE

This means unconquerable, too great to overcome, problems that are overwhelming; issues that are invincible, impossible to fix and insuperable.

How to use this word

You could say:

- 'I feel as though I am facing *insurmountable* difficulties regarding the repayments on my loans and credit cards, and so would really appreciate some help.'

When talking to someone who's worried about a big problem, you could comfort him or her by saying:

- 'These are not *insurmountable* issues – I'm sure we can work them out.'

Maybe at work when there are a lot of challenges, you might say:

- 'The seemingly *insurmountability* of these problems is my next challenge. I will take one problem at a time and fix it.'

And finally . . .

It is pronounced **in-sir-MOUNT-abul**, with the emphasis on the **MOUNT** part of the word.

INTERMITTENT

This is just a fancy word for irregular, stop-start, now and again, on-off-on-off-on-off – those types of words and meanings. Think of the word 'intermission' (interval at the theatre), and you will see how this word works. 'To intermit' means to suspend. All these words are derived from the Latin word intermittere ('leave off', 'let go').

How to use this word

You can describe something as *intermittent.* For example:

- 'These payments are *intermittent* (or my bouts of depression are *intermittent*).'

You could also say:

- 'I have been paying off my overdraft in *intermittent* instalments of £10 here and £10 there.'

And finally . . .

It's similar to the term 'ad hoc', the difference being 'ad hoc' means from time to time with no guarantees of coming back, whereas *intermittently* is more on-off-on-off-on-off. When saying this word, note that the emphasis is on the second syllable: **inter-MITT-unt**.

INTRINSIC

This means being a vital part; an element or a characteristic of something or someone; belonging to something as one of the main elements that make it exist. Actually, it's easier than it sounds.* See the examples below and make sure you read the footnote – it's an intrinsic part of this!

How to use this word

For example:

- 'On-the-job training is an *intrinsic* part of becoming a good customer services rep.'
- 'Josie works 60 hours a week. Non-stop grafting is an *intrinsic* part of her character.'

Perhaps when complaining to a store you could say:

- 'You left out the CD-ROM when I bought the computer and it's an *intrinsic* part of the kit.'

And finally . . .

It is pronounced **in-TRINS-ick**, harder on the **TRINS** part.
I reckon if you just use intrinsic where you'd put basic, you'll be OK.

IRASCIBLE

This word refers to someone who quickly becomes angry and hot-tempered, someone who is known for his or her anger. It also means touchy, testy, irritable, hot-tempered. It comes from the Latin word ira ('anger', 'wrath').

How to use this word

If someone snaps at you, then tell him or her not to be so *irascible*. You can talk about an *irascible* old man, for example, or someone with an *irascible* nature.

Alternatively, you could say:

- 'It's difficult to work with Michelle because she so *irascible*.'
- 'The more successful he becomes, the more *irascible* he gets.'

And finally . . .

When saying this word, it is pronounced **ir-RASS-ibul**, with the emphasis on the second syllable.

IRREVERENT

This refers to someone who is discourteous, disrespectful, impudent, cheeky, impolite, mocking, impious. In the context of talking about a person, it takes the rude angle. In a religious context, it takes the disrespectful angle.

How to use this word

You could say:

- 'I am offended by your *irreverent* attitude towards me, and would like you to leave.'

- 'I find the jokes about my religion *irreverent* and in bad taste.'

In a letter of complaint you might write:

- 'I think your workers have an *irreverent* manner towards their customers.'

Or

- 'Allowing a kebab van in the church car park is an *irreverent* use of church property.'

And finally . . .

It is pronounced **ir-REV-errunt**, heavy on the **REV** part.

JEJUNE

This refers to someone who is simple, childish, naïve, dull, tame, unsophisticated, immature, unsatisfying to the mind, irreverent. The spirit of the word is that of someone chatting away in a boring manner about something beyond his or her intellectual capabilities. It comes from the Latin word jejunus ('empty stomach', 'fasting').

How to use this word

You could say:

- 'The woman at the party was *jejunely* talking about international finances and, as a result, I practically fell asleep… straight into her drink!'
- 'He made a *jejune* generalisation about teachers working only half the year because of all their long holidays.'
- 'The *jejuneness* of the conversation with the office junior about where the company should be going went on for what seemed an eternity.'

And finally . . .

It is pronounced **ji-JOON**, with the **JOON** part of the word slightly harder.

JOCOSE

This is a lovely happy word, nice and positive; it means merry, jovial, jolly, funny, humorous, cheerful, playful. The opposite of this word is melancholy.

How to use this word

You could say:

- 'I was most impressed by the *jocose* nature of the staff at the play centre – the children had a wonderful time.'
- 'I'm sorry, but I am not in a very *jocose* mood today. I'm just feeling a little melancholy.'
- 'Today is Monday – that's why I am not looking very *jocose*.'
- 'The atmosphere there is so *jocose* that I actually came away feeling very happy indeed!'

And finally . . .

When I was writing this at three in the morning, I certainly wasn't in a very jocose mood, definitely more melancholic. It is pronounced **juh-COSE**, emphasising the **COSE** part.

KLEPTOMANIA

This word refers to someone who is obsessed with stealing and who has an overwhelming desire to steal what does not belong to him or her – often items for which he or she has no real need. Kleptomania is considered to be a mental illness, not a description of someone who steals for a laugh or because he or she wants something he or she can't afford. It comes from the Greek word kleptes ('thief').

How to use this word

This is quite simple to use. For example:

- 'You are a *kleptomaniac*. You seem to have a problem stealing a lot of things for which you really have no need at all.'

In this case you would describe someone as having *kleptomania*.

You can also describe someone as having a tendency towards *kleptomania*.

And finally . . .

It is pronounced **klept-ta-MAIN-ee-a**, with the emphasis on **MAIN**.

KOWTOW

At last, I've found an interesting and unusual word beginning with the letter K! It means to bow, grovel, scrape and, yep, we've all worked with someone on whom we can use this word!

How to use this word

You could say:

- 'I am not *kowtowing* to the new boss and his ridiculous demands.'
- 'Adam said he will *kowtow* to him because he needs the money.'
- 'And I *kowtowed* to him all day – he seemed to enjoy it.'

And finally . . .

It's interesting to note that kowtow was once a Chinese gesture – people dropped to their knees and touched the ground with their foreheads to show respect. Now the word metaphorically (see page 104) refers to someone who does that! It is pronounced **COW-TOW**, with equal stress on each syllable. It's said **COW** as in 'moo' and **TOW** as in 'town' but without the 'n'.

LACONIC

This word is of Greek origin and it is used to describe someone who is terse, concise and of few words, or someone who uses words economically. In ancient Greece, the city of Sparta was in Laconia, whose inhabitants were well known for their brevity of speech.

How to use this word

You could say:

- 'I found the sales staff friendly but rather *laconic*. I think you should have more information in store or better trained staff.'

In other words, they weren't rude but didn't say much.

Another example would be:

- 'The youth leader is a nice man but he's so *laconic*, I'm not sure whether he's shy or just doesn't like me.'

Here, the youth leader is being brief or to the point – he does not make additional conversation or offer to help.

And finally . . .

The emphasis is on the second syllable of the word, which is pronounced **la-CON-ik**.

LITIGIOUS

This refers to someone who is prepared to take legal action if necessary; someone keen on litigation; someone who is more likely to use the law to protect him or herself. It comes from the Latin word litigo ('quarrel').

How to use this word

You could say:

- 'We are becoming *litigiously* aware as a nation due to the compensation culture in which we now live.'
- 'Britain is arguably as *litigious* as the USA with so many firms advertising a "no win, no fee" service.'
- 'That actress is *litigious* by nature, and so the journalists are cautious when they write about her.'

And finally . . .

When saying this word, it is pronounced **li-TIJ-uss**, with the emphasis on the second syllable. The third letter 'i' is not heard.

LUGUBRIOUS

This means gloomy, depressing, mournful, sad, sombre, cheerless, gloomy, fed up. Lugubrious is sad and melancholy in a serious way. It comes from the Latin word lugere ('mourn').

How to use this word

You could say, for example:

- 'She had a *lugubrious* face after hearing she'd lost her job.'

If complaining:

- 'I felt the sales assistant served us *lugubriously* and reluctantly.'
- 'The *lugubriousness* of the reception staff didn't make a very good impression when we arrived at the resort.'

And finally . . .

It is pronounced **lug-GOO-bree-us**, with the emphasis on the second syllable.

MAGNANIMOUS

This word means a big-hearted, noble gesture; worthy; of immense generosity; kind, charitable and unselfish. It comes from the Latin words magnus ('great') and animus ('mind', 'spirit').

How to use this word

You could say, for example:

- 'The losing team at the athletics ground was *magnanimous* in defeat and praised their competitors on their victory.'
- 'The Chairman of the company *magnanimously* donated a thousand pounds to the local hospice.'
- 'Hilary was *magnanimous* in forgiving the friend who had refused to speak to her for so many years.'

And finally . . .

Magnanimous is not just generosity of the wallet but also of the heart, and it always refers to something big and eyebrow raising! Make sure you emphasise the second syllable, **mag-NAN-ee-mus**.

MALAPROPISM

This means the incorrect use of a word due to its similarity to another word, especially when the resulting effect is ridiculous. Its origin can be traced back to a Restoration comedy character called Mrs Malaprop, in Sheridan's The Rivals, who tripped up on some of her sayings.

How to use this word

Here are two great examples of *malapropisms*:

- 'The Virgin Mary was also known as the Immaculate Contraption' (instead of the Immaculate Conception).
- 'Baby Jesus was given gifts of gold, myrrh and Frankenstein.'

And finally . . .

Children are often a great, innocent source of malapropisms, as are those who are trying to impress by using 'Big Words' without enlisting the help of *The Little Book of Big Words*! It is pronounced **MAL-la-prop-iz-um**, making sure the emphasis is on the first syllable.

MALEVOLENT

This means spiteful, vicious, evil, wicked, intending to do harm, nasty, mean, full of hate. Other definitions of this word are vindictive, vengeful, malicious and resentful. It comes from the Latin word malevolens ('spiteful').

How to use this word

You could say:

- 'She is a *malevolent* old woman, desperate to hurt us one way or another.'
- 'He looked *malevolently* in my direction, with a fixed stare.'
- 'She just wants to be nasty to me. It's sheer *malevolence*.'

And finally . . .

This is pronounced **mal-LEV-a-lent**, with the **LEV** being the strongest sound.

MALIGN

This means to defame, blacken, cause harm, slander, revile, smear, damage, derogate, run down, disparage. It's normally used when your name or character, or that of a business or group, has been reviled.

How to use this word

You could say, for example:

- 'I feel I have been *maligned* in the newspapers with all those nasty remarks.'
- 'I may be much *maligned* for my laid-back style, but I'm quietly getting things done in the background.'
- 'My name has been much *maligned* by those written comments (or spoken words), and I demand an apology.'

And finally . . .

I'm pleased to say that my character was never maligned by any ex-girlfriends! Must be because I'm so nice – that's what my mother says, anyway! It is pronounced **ma-LINE**, emphasising the second half.

MASTICATE

To masticate literally means to chew and grind your teeth well, on food; to pulverise the food in your mouth and to crush it completely.

How to use this word

So if your colleague is being a bit of a pig, or a noisy eater, and you can hear it all, you could say:

- 'There seems to be the sound of serious *mastication* coming from that direction. Nice lunch?'

You could also say:

- 'Despite having some wonderful teeth, the crocodile doesn't bother *masticating* its food – it just swallows it whole.'

- 'I was always taught to chew my food well as a child, almost to the point of *mastication*!'

And finally . . .

Great word but, for obvious reasons, be careful how you say it: be nice and clear, especially when using it as the noun 'mastication'. It is pronounced **MAST-i-kate**, with the emphasis on the first part.

MATUTINAL

This word refers to something that happens first thing in the morning. It comes from the Latin word matutinus ('belonging to the early morning').

How to use this word

If you've been served an appalling breakfast in a hotel, then you could write and complain about the company's substandard *matutinal* food servings.

Maybe you could refer to your flat mate making a noise (gargling and flushing the chain in the morning) as his or her annoying, noisy, *matutinal* routine.

And finally . . .

Don't put the words morning and matutinal together – that would be like putting big and large together – because they mean the same thing! This word is pronounced **ma-CHEW-tin-ul**, with the **CHEW** part of the word sounding strongest.

MEGALOMANIAC

A word that refers to someone who thinks he or she is more important than he or she really is, and who takes an unhealthy delight in displaying his or her power over others; or someone who dreams and exaggerates about how big and powerful he or she is. In other words, the boss! Well some of them, anyway! Megalomaniac comes from the Greek word megas ('great').

How to use this word

You could say, for example:

- 'My boss is a *megalomaniac*.'
- 'He (or she) suffers from *megalomania*.'

And finally . . .

Only say this word if it's true and you can't be heard; otherwise, you could be sued for slander. This word is pronounced **megg-a-la-MAY-knee-ac**, making sure the emphasis is on the fourth syllable.

MELLIFLUOUS

This describes a male or female voice that has a sweet, friendly, polite and well educated tone. It comes from the Latin words mel ('honey') and fluo ('flow').

How to use this word

You could tell someone you like his or her *mellifluous* tones as he or she reads out loud.

You could also say, for example:

- 'I was listening to her *mellifluously* telling me about her tranquil holiday when we were interrupted by the screeching of tyres.'
- 'I like listening to you read (or sing) as the *mellifluousness* of your delivery is so soothing to my ears.'

And finally . . .

Make sure you have the emphasis on the second syllable when you say this word, making it **mel-LIFF-loo-us**.

MEPHITIC

This is another word used to describe a rank, putrid, stinking, foul, disgusting, noxious, unwholesome smell.

How to use this word

You could say:

- 'I approached the end of the garden and came across a nasty, vile, *mephitic* stench, enough to knock someone out.'

- 'Upon our arrival at the holiday camp, we were greeted *mephitically* by the odour of raw sewage.'

Perhaps you could use it when complaining:

- 'When I stayed at your hotel I noticed a *mephitic* stench coming from the basement, which obviously needed urgent investigation.'

And finally . . .

Mephitis is the smell, but when talking about it and describing it, we usually use mephitic and mephitically. I could get on to the subject of teenagers' bedrooms again, but I think they are even worse and should have a set of words of their own, closer to radioactive! It is pronounced **mi-FITT-ick**, with the emphasis on the **FITT**.

MERETRICIOUS

This word means attractive in a vulgar or superficial way; without any real value; seemingly attractive but really quite false and not worth much. It comes from the Latin word meretrix ('prostitute').

How to use this word

While looking around a house that you're thinking of buying, you find it's got a few gaudy extras, like gold taps. You could perhaps say:

- 'There are a few *meretricious* additions that don't really increase the value of the property, so I'm only offering you X pounds.'

The word *meretricious* can also be used to describe an argument, document, letter, newspaper article, etc. For example:

- 'It's a *meretricious* contract.'

In other words, it looks good, but it's worth nothing. You might describe a certain tabloid newspaper you don't like as *meretricious* journalism. In other words, it looks good and flashy, with lots of colour (like the gold taps in the house), but it is not that good when you read it.

And finally . . .

Next time you see a car with a six-foot-high spoiler and furry dice in the front, instead of saying 'What a moron', say: 'That's such a meretricious-looking car' – unless you actually like that kind of thing. It is pronounced **merra-TRISH-us**, harder on the **TRISH** part.

METAPHORICALLY

This is an interesting, simple word to use or understand and one that drops perfectly into conversation. A metaphor is a term used when making a comparison that is not meant to be taken at face value. It's basically a figure of speech used to paint a picture and to make a statement more visual or exciting. Metaphors can be ridiculously dramatic at times.

How to use this word

A great example of a *metaphor* is the term: 'You scratch my back and I'll scratch yours.' Nobody is scratching anybody's back at all. It just means you do me a favour and I'll do you one. It's a *metaphor*. You could say:

- '*Metaphorically* speaking, I'm going to scratch your back.'

Remember when you warned someone that, if he or she didn't do something, he or she would be in deep sh…? Well, that's speaking *metaphorically*. You often tag the words 'speaking *metaphorically*' on to the end of just such a statement to point out that you don't really mean it. You could say, for example:

- 'I could kiss you all over, *metaphorically* speaking.'

In other words, I'm exaggerating to show you how I feel.

And finally . . .

Don't confuse metaphors with similes, which use words to compare things. Examples include 'as high as a kite' and 'as daft as a brush'. It is pronounced **metta-FORRI-klee**, with the emphasis on the middle of the word, syllables 3 and 4.

METATHESIS

This is a rarely used word but worth knowing. I've heard it mentioned a few times in discussion. It refers to the transposition of letters or sounds in a word that have swapped around. Some examples may include the Old English word 'brid', becoming 'bird', 'hros' becoming 'hors' and 'flutter-by' becoming 'butterfly'. The word metathesis comes from the Greek word 'metatithenai', meaning 'transpose'.

How to use this word

You can say:

- 'Did you know the word hros changed to horse through *metathesis*.'

This same process is responsible for the word 'lisp'. It was once spelt 'wlips' and the letters changed around. In Old English the word 'wlips' meant lisping, speaking inarticulately or with a stammer. That's why there's an unfortunate letter 's' in the word lisp.

Metathesis may not be a word you will use every day, but as this is a book of unusual words, it's good to know how some of them have come about.

And finally . . .

It is pronounced **metta-THEE-seez**, harder on the middle of the word.

MOLLIFY

This means to pacify, calm, soothe, placate or appease someone. In other words, calm someone down after he or she has been angry. It comes from the Latin word mollis ('soft').

How to use this word

You could say in a letter of complaint:

- 'My husband was angry because there were a lot of hairs and fingernails in the shower in our hotel room. I had to *mollify* him before ringing reception to ask for it to be sorted it out.'

You could also say:

- 'I *mollified* the situation by suggesting that we did (this, that or the other).'

- 'After a terrible week, I had to *mollify* my boss by reminding her of last week's great sales figures before we could proceed.'

And finally . . .

This is pronounced **MOLL-if-eye**, emphasising the first part.

MONOMANIA

This word refers to a mental fixation or obsession with something in particular. In other words, you can use it when you've got a thing about this or a bee in your bonnet about that. Mono, of course, indicates 'one thing', as in monorail and monotonous.

How to use this word

You could say:

- 'Mum's a bit of a *monomaniac* when it comes to keeping the kitchen tidy, so please wash up after yourself, Aaron!'
- 'I'm afraid it's a case of *monomania* when you borrow one of my books. You must look after it, because I hate it when books are scruffy.'
- 'My friend won't let anyone in the house with their shoes on. He's a real *monomaniac* when it comes to this.'
- 'Kristian's a *monomaniac* when it comes to the Simpsons. He's always watching it and his room is full of Simpsons' memorabilia.'

And finally . . .

It is pronounced **mono-MAY-nia**.

MONOSYLLABICALLY

This word refers to someone who makes conversation using words consisting of just one syllable. The spirit of the word really refers to someone who answers with one or two words and makes no further comment or effort at conversation. That's most teenagers, then!

How to use this word

Gareth says: 'How are you today, Harry?', who answers *monosyllabically* with: 'Fine.' Harry is now technically *monosyllabic*. He's talking using just one syllable. You can tell someone he or she is *monosyllabic* if that person just answers 'yes' or 'no', or with a very short answer. You could say, therefore:

- 'Can you expand on that *monosyllabic* answer?'

Or, by making your comments to others:

- 'Harry is in a mood – he's just answering *monosyllabically*.'

- 'I did try to get the appropriate information from the sales girl, but she was rather *monosyllabic*.'

And finally . . .

Most teenage boys are monosyllabic (if a grunt counts!). How ironic that a word meaning 'using words of just one syllable' actually has six syllables itself! There goes that weird English language again. It is pronounced **monna-sil-LAB-ik-lee**, using the **LAB** part as the hardest syllable.

MONOTHEISM

This word refers to the belief in just one God. It's not referring to any single religion, just how we believe – i.e. a belief that there is one god only. The first part of the word is 'mono' – i.e. 'one' (think monocycle, monorail, monotonous). 'Theism' comes from the Greek word theos ('god').

How to use this word

You can say:

- 'Catholicism is one of the largest *monotheistic* religions.'
- '*Monotheism* generally seems to be the popular form of faith.'
- 'I have *monotheistic* beliefs.'
- 'I have been praying and believing *monotheistically* all my life.'

And finally . . .

Not a word you'd probably use a lot, but good to understand. I've heard it mentioned a few times on the television. It is pronounced **monna-THEE-iz-um**, emphasising the **THEE** part.

MORDANT

This word means a sarcastic, critical or biting remark – one that's scathingly caustic and penetrating.

How to use this word

So, if someone attacks you with a sharp tongue, you could say:

- 'That was a very *mordant* remark!'

Or

- 'With comments like that it proves your *mordancy* knows no limits.'

You could also accuse someone of *mordantly* trying to put you down.

And finally . . .

This is also the name of a chemical, but the context in which you use the word will make it self-explanatory. It is easy to pronounce. Just emphasise the first part of the word: **MORE-dunt**.

MUNIFICENT

An interesting word that means generous, bountiful, liberal, open-handed, free-handed, magnanimous (see page 94), unstinting. It can be used to describe a character of immense generosity, one displaying a giving nature. It comes from the Latin word munus ('gift').

How to use this word

You could say:

- 'Marian has *munificently* given us this gift. How kind of her, don't you think?'
- 'In a great show of *munificence*, my boss has agreed to give me a 50 per cent pay rise.'
- 'My boss is so *munificent*, he's increased my wages by 50 per cent. I could hug him! It was such a magnanimous (see page 94) gesture.'

And finally . . .

Concerning the free copy of this book I have given to my boss – please take special note of examples 2 and 3 (except the hugging part!). It is pronounced **mew-NIFF-is-unt**, with the **NIFF** the strongest-sounding part.

MYRIAD

This is a colourful word used to say 'a great number' of something. Today, although it has lost its literal meaning, it still sounds far more sophisticated than 'loads of'. It comes from the Latin murioi ('ten thousand', 'innumerable', 'countless').

How to use this word

You could say, for example:

- 'There always seems to be a *myriad* of choices when trying to make a decision over something important.'
- 'There's a *myriad* of colours staring back at me when I look at the many differently coloured paints in the hardware store.'

And finally . . .

By the way, don't confuse this word with a well-known computer program called *Myriad* – probably so called because it can do 10,000 different things for you. It is pronounced **MIRRY-add**, emphasising the first part of the word.

NEBULOUS

Nebulous means hazy, misty, cloudy, ill-defined, imprecise, vague, cloudy, or cloud-like, shapeless, obscure – in other words, just not very clear!

How to use this word

You could say:

- 'He has a few *nebulous* ideas about how he wants to redesign the house, but nothing very clear.'
- 'You have promised to compensate me for mis-selling, but so far I've only had a few *nebulous* suggestions made to me.'
- 'The *nebulousness* of the contract indicates that a further meeting between us is now necessary.'
- 'This *nebulous* credit agreement indicates I must pay by the 12th of each month, but the figures don't add up. Please take a look.'

And finally . . .

Is that clear? Or is it a nebulous explanation of the word? It is pronounced **NEB-yoo-lus**, emphasising the **NEB**.

NEFARIOUS

This means extremely wicked, immoral and utterly evil. I can think of a few people to whom I could attribute this word! It comes from the Latin word nefas ('not divine').

How to use this word

You could say:

- 'I don't like to get involved with Jake because of his *nefarious* activities and comments.'
- 'The gang was involved in robbery, drugs, violence and a number of other *nefarious* activities.'
- 'The boys on the street corner have been picking *nefariously* on passers-by, often in a violent manner.'

And finally . . .

Here's a good one: you could accuse someone who's being nasty of having a nefarious tongue. That'll shut him or her up! It is pronounced **ni-FAIR-ree-us**,
with the emphasis on **FAIR**.

NETTLESOME

Here's a strange word, and it's got nothing to do with nettles at all but is used to describe something that's irritating or distressing to you in some way.

How to use this word

You can talk about a number of *nettlesome* issues or about problems that need addressing or solving. It's as simple as that! Pretend you're swapping the word irritating for the word *nettlesome*.

For example, when writing to the bank you could say:

- 'I know that being overdrawn two days before pay day every month is a *nettlesome* subject that needs looking at as soon as possible.'

If you're complaining about somebody at work, you might want to say:

- 'His constant swearing in the office is a *nettlesome* issue that I need to bring to your attention.'

And finally . . .

It's a little used word that really makes people sit up and take notice – a bit like sitting on nettles, really! It is pronounced **NETT-ul-sum**, emphasising the first syllable.

NONCHALANT

This refers to someone who is dispassionate, unconcerned, not bothered, blasé, apathetic, cool, casual, laid-back, indifferent, detached, calm, easy, carefree. It tends to be used in a negative manner. It comes from the French word nonchalior ('unconcerned').

How to use this word

When complaining you could say:

- 'The waiters *nonchalantly* brought out the food, without any sense of urgency or excitement.'

Or

- 'They brought the food out with such *nonchalance*.'

You might also say:

- 'My son mows the lawn for me with such *nonchalance* that I may as well do it myself: it would be quicker and I would probably achieve better results.'
- 'I find you rather *nonchalant* in your attitude and really need to see a bit of spark in you.'

And finally . . .

This is pronounced **NON-shul-unt**, emphasising the first syllable.

OBDURATE

This means to be hard-hearted, cold, harsh, inflexible, stubborn, head strong, unfeeling, callous, not likely to feel sympathy, inflexible, pig-headed, unbending; a refusal to change an opinion no matter what. It can be applied to someone who is completely immovable. It comes from the Latin word durus ('hard').

How to use this word

There is a family feud, which goes back years, and for that reason Michael won't go to Uncle Bartholomew's funeral. As a result you could say:

- 'Michael is completely *obdurate* and refuses to go to the funeral.'

Or

- 'He is *obdurately* refusing to go.'

You might also perhaps say:

- 'My boss remains *obdurate* about not giving a pay rise for the second year running, despite everyone struggling financially.'

- 'The manager of the football team remains *obdurate* that no wives or girlfriends are allowed to travel with the players during the Cup Final.'

And finally . . .

It is pronounced **OB-jur-ut**, with the emphasis on the **OB** part of the word.

OBFUSCATE

This word is so relevant to this book it's amazing! It refers to the smarmy people who use long words to try to confuse you. The whole point of this book is to learn those very words so that you don't look ignorant, or so that you yourself can, in fact, throw them into a conversation or correspondence to prove that you are indeed as intelligent as they. The actual meaning of this word is intentionally to make things more confusing. It comes from the Latin word fuscus ('dark').

How to use this word

You could use it in a disagreement when someone throws in irrelevant matters by saying:

- 'You're just *obfuscating* the main issue by bringing in other irrelevant matters.'

In other words, by bringing into the argument a lot of other issues, it has become too complicated and confusing:

- 'I am accusing the supplier of obstruction and *obfuscation* by not providing the right documents and by supplying many others that we don't need.'

And finally . . .

To recap, if someone is obfuscating, he or she is making it less clear to understand – on purpose! It is pronounced **OB-fus-kate**, with the emphasis on the first syllable.

OBJURGATE

This word means to berate, rebuke, scold, reprimand, denounce, reproach, castigate, chide. It is the opposite of praise. It comes from the Latin word jurgium ('quarrel').

How to use this word

You could say:

- 'At work, our department received a severe *objurgation* after we missed our sales target yet again.'
- 'I was *objurgated* by a policeman for not wearing my seat belt, but he let me off with a warning.' (As if!)
- 'The staff should have been *objurgated* for giving such bad service to their customers.'

And finally . . .

Think of 'to objurgate' as 'to tell off severely' and you won't go far wrong. It is pronounced as read.

OBSEQUIOUS

This word refers to someone who is smarmy, submissive, flattering and creepy towards others. It is quite similar to sycophantic (see page 173). It comes from the Latin word obsequor ('comply with').

How to use this word

You can simply say:

- 'Peter was very *obsequious* around the boss at the company dinner, wasn't he?'

Or

- 'I noticed how Peter was *obsequiously* supplying plenty of wine to the Directors and generally running around after them.'

You might also say:

- 'I hate working with George – he's so *obsequious*.'

And finally . . .

Yep, we've all worked with a George! Now you've got a better way to describe him! It's a negative word – not very nice. So don't use it to describe someone who's being helpful. It's pronounced **ob-SEE-kewee-us**, with the emphasis on the second syllable.

OBSTREPEROUS

This word refers to someone who resists and fights against those in authority, someone who doesn't like to be given orders or controlled, which often makes his or her behaviour unruly. It means aggressive, bad-tempered, hostile, defiant, argumentative, loud, turbulent, wild, out-of-hand, unmanageable, disorderly.

How to use this word

You could say:

- 'My teenage son is behaving *obstreperously* at school and will have to be put in a special class if this behaviour doesn't improve.'
- 'Whenever I deal with my ex-wife she seems to be *obstreperous* towards me, making it difficult to have a reasonable discussion about the children and money matters.'
- 'When I was serving in the shop today, we seemed to have a few *obstreperous* customers.'

And finally . . .

It is pronounced **ob-STREP-per-us**, with the emphasis on the **STREP**.

OCTOGENARIAN

This word describes someone who is in his or her eighties. Octogenarian comes from the Latin word octogenarius ('eighty').

How to use this word

You could say you have a couple of *octogenarians* living next door.

You can also refer to someone in his or her seventies as septuagenarians, although that seems to be rarely used in comparison with *octogenarian*.

You might also say:

- 'We're proud of Uncle Bob for, despite his ill-health, tomorrow he becomes the only *octogenarian* in the family.'

And finally . . .

When saying this word, it is pronounced **octo-jen-AIR-ee-un**, emphasising the **AIR** part.

ODIOUS

This word means to arouse a strong dislike, revulsion, aversion, repugnance or intense displeasure. It comes from the Latin word odium ('hatred').

How to use this word

You can describe someone as a mean and *odious* old man. You could also say something along the lines of:

- 'You *odious* little man – sitting there criticising my every action.'

You could also say:

- 'There is an *odious* smell coming from the bathroom.'

You can refer to items or situations as being *odious*. For example, 'the *odious* debts of the third world increase hunger' or 'the decorations in that house were truly *odious*'.

And finally . . .

This is pronounced **OH-dee-us**, making the **OH** the strongest part of the word.

ONOMATOPOEIA

A lovely word used to describe a word that's made up of the sound it literally makes – a vocal imitation, as it were!

Great examples include:

- buzz
- cuckoo
- murmur
- pop
- sizzle.

How to use this word
You could say:

- 'I think I know what that word means because of its *onomatopoeic* connotations.'

You could also announce that a word is *onomatopoeically* explained (i.e. by the sound).

And finally . . .

This is not a word that is used often but another that's bound to come up in a pub quiz one day! It is pronounced **ono-mat-OPE-ee-a**, emphasising the **OPE** part of the word.

OPULENT

This means an abundant, luxurious display, or an exhibition of wealth and affluence. In other words, plenty of money! You would use this word to describe a place that was lavishly furnished, in a manner that was somewhat over the top. It comes from the Latin word opulentus ('wealthy', 'splendid').

How to use this word

You could say, for example:

- 'The gold, 24-foot-high fountain stands *opulently* at the front of the house.'
- 'The *opulence* of the design increases the value of the property, or shows that the owners have good taste.'
- 'She walked through the rough neighbourhood with a diamond necklace *opulently* hanging around her neck.' (Actually, I would say 'stupidly' hanging round her neck here!)

And finally . . .

This is not a negative word and it won't offend because it signifies tasteful wealth. Sadly, it's a word that will never be used to describe my little house in Buckinghamshire! It is pronounced **OPP-you-lunt**, emphasising the **OPP** part.

OSTENTATIOUS

A word meaning a flashy, tacky, vulgar display of wealth, designed to impress others. Despite its similarity to the word opulent (see page 125), this word is used in a different way. To summarise, opulent refers to a tasteful show of genuine wealth, whereas ostentatious refers to a less-than-tasteful show of wealth, and a show often put on only for the effect it will create.

How to use this word

You could use it to describe someone's house or the clothes that person wears (but just as long as he or she can't hear you!). Perhaps you could say:

- 'They live in a very *ostentatious* house, full of diamond-encrusted plant pots and a 32" TV in every room.'

About the occupier of just such a house, you could also say:

- 'She is a very *ostentatious* dresser – all show and no style.'

And finally . . .

This word is generally used as a criticism, so don't describe your boss's new car as ostentatious – just admire it. Otherwise, you may end up collecting your P45! It is pronounced **os-ten-TAY-shus**, emphasising the **TAY**.

OXYMORON

This word describes two words with totally opposite meanings, brought together jointly to describe one thing. An oxymoron, therefore, contains opposite, contradictory terms. It comes from the Greek words oxus ('sharp') and moros ('dull').

How to use this word

I'm not quite sure where you'd use this word, but I've included it because it's a fascinating one!

Here are some examples of *oxymora*:

- 'Don't worry, we just had a friendly argument – it wasn't serious.'
- 'There was a deafening silence when I walked into the interview room.'
- 'More than a hundred soldiers were killed by friendly fire.'
- 'You clearly misunderstood what I was saying.'

And finally . . .

Note that the plural of oxymoron is oxymora. Makes you look at the English language and think: 'Yep, some of it makes no sense at all!' It is pronounced **oxy-MORE-ron**, with the **MORE** part of the word being emphasised.

PEEVISH

This means fractious, irritable, touchy, crabby, cranky, bad-tempered, cross, querulous, grumpy. In other words, most of us early in the morning!

How to use this word

You could refer to Colin as a bad-tempered, *peevish* man who needs to calm down.

You could also say:

- 'James is *peeved* that you borrowed his book but haven't returned it.'
- 'My teenage son *peevishly* came in at 10 o'clock and then ignored me!'
- 'It *peeves* me that you borrow a fiver every week and never pay it back.'
- 'The boss *peevishly* told us we should have given him more help with the project.'

And finally . . .

When saying this word, the emphasis should be on the **PEE** part: **PEE-vish**.

PERENNIAL

This refers to something that lasts a long time, or keeps happening over and over again; constant, persistent, returning, lasting, continuing, recurring. It comes from the Latin word perennis ('everlasting', 'uninterrupted').

How to use this word

You could say, for example:

- 'There is the *perennial* problem of having no babysitter at the weekends, just when we need to work.'
- 'Mum's Sunday lunch is a *perennial* treat and one we always enjoy.'
- 'The film, *The Wizard of Oz*, is the *perennial* favourite and one we watch on the TV every festive season.'

And finally . . .

My tax bill is a perennial treat I look forward to every January – yeah, right! It is pronounced **per-RENN-ial**, with the emphasis on the **RENN** part.

PERFIDIOUS

This means disloyal, deceitful, dishonest, base, unfaithful, untrustworthy, traitorous, false, lying, two-faced. Perfidy comes from the Latin word perfidia ('treachery', 'faithlessness').

How to use this word

You could say:

- 'Alistair being unfaithful was a *perfidious* attack on our marriage.'
- 'I consider your *perfidious* actions contrary to the interests of this company. You're fired!'
- 'Alistair has been *perfidiously* seeing the woman next door and sneaking off for days out.'
- 'The fact that the political party for whom I voted decided not to lower taxes as promised is proof of the hypocrisy and *perfidy* of politicians.'

And finally . . .

When you say this word, it is pronounced **per-FIDD-ee-us**, with the emphasis on the **FIDD** part.

PERFUNCTORY

This describes something that is done mechanically, routinely and without much passion, care or interest; something that's done out of duty. It comes from the Latin word perfungi ('get through', 'perform').

How to use this word

Maybe when complaining you might say:

- 'I reported the fault to a customer services representative who took down the details in a *perfunctory* manner.'

You might perhaps say to someone who's listening to you, but obviously not taking in a word you're saying:

- 'Don't sit there in that *perfunctory* way.'

You could also say:

- 'My mother-in-law kisses me in the usual *perfunctory* way when we visit, but I know she doesn't really like me.'

And finally . . .

Make sure you emphasise the **FUNK** part of this word in conversation: **per-FUNK-tur-ee**.

PERNICKETY

This word describes someone who is over-precise, a perfectionist; someone who is fussy about the smallest of details. It's neither a negative nor a positive word on its own, for it is the context or the way in which it is used that would sway it one way or the other.

How to use this word

You could tell someone, for example, who spends hours getting the creases in a pleated skirt just right when she irons that she's *pernickety*.

You could describe the man next door as *pernickety* about his lawn because he trims the edges with scissors.

Alternatively, you could describe someone as generally *pernickety* – in other words, someone who pays enormous attention to detail.

And finally . . .

In conversation, this should be pronounced **per-NICK-at-ee**, with the emphasis on the **NICK** part of the word.

PERQUISITE

This word usually refers to a perk, benefit or allowance given on top of a regular income.

How to use this word

You could say, for example, that the salary for your new job is much better, and that a company car and profit share are also a *perquisite* of the overall package.

You may read that laptops were once the *perquisite* of the managers, but now we all get them so that we can work anywhere and achieve more.

You may want to argue:

- 'This tool is not a *perquisite* of my job – it's a necessity if you want the job doing to your standard, so don't withdraw it, please.'

And finally . . .

Think of it as a substitute for the word 'benefit' and you won't go far wrong. It is pronounced **purr-QUIZ-it**, with the emphasis on the **QUIZ** part of the word.

PERSPICUOUS

A word used to describe something that's expressed and explained in a clear and concise manner without confusion.

How to use this word

You could, for example, complain that the small print on a contract isn't very *perspicuous*.

You could also declare that something had been *perspicuously* explained to you so that you could understand it.

You might say that someone talks with *perspicacity*, because he or she always expresses him or herself clearly, giving clear and concise explanations.

And finally . . .

In other words, this can be attributed to someone who makes him or herself clearly understood. Make sure you emphasise the **SPICK** part of the word when you say it: **per-SPICK-you-us**.

PERUSE

This refers to someone who is looking through or reading something leisurely, but carefully. It is a simple, but often forgotten word. The common mistake is to use the word when meaning 'a quick flick or read-through'. In fact it is the exact opposite, being a detailed look at something.

How to use this word

You might say:

- 'I *perused* the newspaper this morning but can't find anything interesting at all.'
- 'On that story you want to hear about… Did you have time for a *perusal*?'
- 'After *perusing* this legal document, I think I need more time to look at it again.'
- 'Did you have time to *peruse* the document (or brochure or letter) I sent you?' (Meaning, have you looked at it in detail?)

And finally . . .

When you say this word, you should emphasise the second syllable (and make it last!): **per-OOOZE.**

PETULANT

This means bad-tempered, ill-tempered, snappy, grouchy, impatient, irritable, peevish, childishly angry. It comes from the Latin word petere ('demand', 'request').

How to use this word

Try this:

- 'The waiters who served us were rather *petulant*, which spoiled the evening.'

You could say *petulantly*:

- 'He didn't invite me to his wedding, so he's not coming to mine.'

You could also say:

- 'Stop being so *petulant* about this issue. We need to take a mature attitude to resolve it.'

And finally . . .

The key to this word is to remember that it is a childish way of being annoyed – another word to describe those teenagers. When saying this word, the emphasis should be on the first syllable: **PET-you-lunt**.

PHARISAIC

This is a word that can be used in place of one of my favourite words, 'sanctimonious'. Like sanctimonious, it means self-righteous and holier-than-thou. It can be used to describe someone who looks down his or her nose at another person.

How to use this word

You can say:

- 'Don't be so *pharisaical* about my white lie: you tell enough white lies yourself!'

When someone criticises you, and looks down on you for doing something, you could say:

- 'That's a very *pharisaic* remark. Don't judge me – I do what I think is best.'

Or

- 'Don't be so *pharisaic*, Harriett.'

And finally . . .

If you're not familiar with this word, just remember to use it when someone looks down on you for doing something when he or she has no right to judge you at all. This word has the emphasis on the **SAY** part of the word when you say it: **farra-SAY-ick**.

PHLEGMATIC

This word means lethargic, sluggish, lazy-like, indifferent, disinterested, not agitated, showing a slow temperament, apathetic.

How to use this word

You could say:

- 'The boss's *phlegmatic* manner is one of his less attractive personality traits.'
- 'I have a fifteen-year-old boy who just seems to mope *phlegmatically* around the house during the school holidays.'
- 'The staff seemed to be dealing with the customers in a rather *phlegmatic* way, which was inappropriate because there were a lot of us trying to book into the hotel.'

And finally . . .

In conversation, the emphasis is on the second syllable: **flegg-MATT-ik**.

PHOBIA

A phobia is an excessive and irrational fear of something. Everyone knows agoraphobia is a fear of open spaces and claustrophobia is a fear of confined spaces, but here are a few of the lesser known phobias.

- *Catoptrophobia*: fear of mirrors.
- *Gamophobia*: fear of getting married.
- *Hominophobia*: fear of men.
- *Kathisophobia*: fear of sitting down.
- *Pyrophobia*: fear of fire.
- *Rhytiphobia*: fear of getting wrinkles.
- *Venustraphobia*: fear of beautiful women.

And finally . . .

The word 'phobia' should not be used to describe the sort of fear we all occasionally feel, be it of snakes or spiders, for example. A 'real' phobia is a fear that is out of control and that dictates how the sufferer may lead his or her life. It is a debilitating fear. When saying this word, the emphasis is on the first syllable: **FOE-be-a**.

PLACATE

This means to calm down, soothe, mollify, pacify, conciliate, appease. It comes from the Latin word placare ('calm').

How to use this word

You might say, for example:

- 'The sales assistant offered me a credit note in an attempt to *placate* me, but I wasn't happy with that.'
- 'To *placate* your customers, perhaps you should do (this, that or the other).'
- 'I wasn't *placated* with the offer of a replacement.'
- 'Perhaps an offer of a full refund would have been a more *placatory* solution.'

And finally . . .

This is pronounced **play-KATE**, with the emphasis on the second syllable.

PLAINTIVE

This means sad, mournful, doleful, melancholic, lamenting, heart rendering, sorrowful. It's not to be confused with the similar-looking word 'plaintiff', meaning prosecutor.

How to use this word

You could say:

- 'I found the plot of the film extremely *plaintive* – it made me want to cry.'
- 'Aisha left her job on the last day and *plaintively* said goodbye to everybody.'
- 'In the hotel, the *plaintive* sound of the piano in the bar made me think about the old days.'
- 'The *plaintiveness* of the funeral was just too much for Harold, and he burst into tears.'

And finally . . .

When saying this word, it is pronounced **PLANE-tiv**, making sure the emphasis is on the first syllable.

PLATEAU

This word means 'a state of stability' – a situation where there's no change, variation or movement.

How to use this word

You could say, for example:

- 'My club membership kept increasing year after year until it finally reached a *plateau* about two years ago.'
- 'I've been losing two or three pounds a week on this new diet, but for the last few weeks I've lost nothing. I must have reached the infamous dieter's *plateau*, neither gaining nor losing anything.'
- 'Interest rates slowly crept up last year, but now they seem to have reached a *plateau* and are far more stable.'
- 'I have been increasing the time I spend jogging by 10 minutes every day, but I think I've reached a *plateau* at 90 minutes.'

And finally . . .

This is pronounced **platt-OW**, with the emphasis on the second syllable. And it's **OW** as in 'row' and not **OW** as in 'cow'.

PLETHORA

This word refers to an excess, surplus, over-abundance; too much or a surfeit of something – way too much, more than you could possibly ever need. The opposite of this word is dearth.

How to use this word

You could say:

- 'Since we had cable TV put in, we have a *plethora* of new channels.'
- 'The library has a *plethora* of books on surnames, but not on baby names, which is what I need.'
- 'A *plethoric* selection of radio channels on my new digital set is confusing me, but I do appreciate the choice.'
- 'There was a *plethora* of food at the Christmas party – too much for such a small company.'

And finally . . .

I have a plethora of credit cards all up to the limit, so I'm pleased you've bought this book! This is pronounced **PLETH-arra**, making sure the emphasis is on the first part, **PLETH**.

PRIMA FACIE

This literally means on the face of it, at first glance, at the first view, on first impression. We often talk about something being prima facie evidence of this, that and the other.

How to use this word

You could complain to a company that, when you spotted its interest rates were just 5 per cent, that was *prima facie* evidence of a good deal, but you have since discovered that all is not what it first appeared.

You could also say:

- '*Prima facie*, the jumper in the sale for £5 seemed a real bargain, but now all the stitching has come out I feel robbed!'
- 'The *prime facie* evidence was less than convincing, so the police could not charge the suspect.'

And finally . . .

Don't ruin it all, though, by pronouncing it incorrectly! This word should be pronounced **pree-ma-FAY-shee**, emphasising the third syllable.

PROBITY

This means with goodness, decency, honesty, integrity, honour, virtue, morality, truthfulness, uprightness, principle, virtue. It comes from the Latin word probus ('good').

How to use this word

You could say:

- 'Some of his finer qualities are his *probity* and reliability.'
- 'His speech was delivered with such *probity* that it really was a joy to listen to him.'
- 'Vera's *probity* was one of her finer characteristics: she was such an honourable lady.'

And finally . . .

When saying this word, put the emphasis on the first syllable: **PROW-bitty**. The **PROW** rhymes with 'owe' (as in 'owe money').

PROCRASTINATE

Procrastinate means to put off doing something until later. It comes from the Latin word cras ('of tomorrow').

How to use this word

If your son, for example, keeps telling you that he will sort out something tomorrow because he is too busy today, then you could say: 'Stop *procrastinating*!'

Or you could accuse him of being a *procrastinator* and remind him of the proverb:

- '*Procrastination* is the thief of time.'

And finally . . .

And if you don't have time to learn this word today, then you could always procrastinate and do it tomorrow, or the day after that… or the day after that… or the day after that! Make sure the emphasis is on the second syllable when you say this word: **pro-CRAST-in-ate**.

PROFANE

This means to treat something religious as unworthy and with a lack of respect, or to treat with contempt.

How to use this word

So you could describe someone's comments about a sacred matter as *profane* or based on *profanity*.

If someone says 'Oh God' in a church or ridicules a religious ceremony he or she is watching on TV, then you could tell that person not to utter such *profanities* in your presence. Or you could say:

- 'We can do without the *profane* remarks, thank you.'

You could also say:

- 'The comedian's opening minute was full of *profanities*; I didn't find it funny at all.'

And finally . . .

This is pronounced **pro-FANE**, with a slight emphasis on the second syllable.

PROFLIGACY

This means extravagant, wasteful, lavish, overspending. The spirit of the word refers to someone who wastes lots of money in a negative way, not to someone who can afford it and who just spends lots of cash.

How to use this word

You could say:

- 'While the ordinary people of this Third World country starve, the *profligacy* of its leaders in their huge palaces has outraged the rest of the world.'
- 'With all their credit cards over the limit, most students are known for their on going *profligate* spending habits.'
- 'Your years of *profligate* spending have resulted in a massive overdraft.'

And finally . . .

When saying this word, it is pronounced **prof-LIGG-ass-ee** – heavy on the **LIGG**!

PROFOUND

This word means deep, intense and serious. It may be used to refer to a statement displaying great insight, study or knowledge.

How to use this word

You can make a *profound* statement or tell people you are going to make a *profound* statement. To say, for example, you are going to give up all meat because you believe it is morally wrong to kill a living creature for human consumption, could be described as a *profound* statement because it is deep and intense, and you have given it a great deal of serious thought.

Similarly, if someone tells you that he or she has a *profound* belief in this, that or the other, that person is saying that his or her belief is deep-rooted and serious.

You can also say:

- 'A *profound* silence fell across the theatre as the main character played out the death scene, revealing the identity of his murderer.'

And finally . . .

When saying this word, make sure you emphasise the second part: **pruf-OUND**. It rhymes with 'sound'.

PROGNOSTICATE

This word means to prophesise, predict, foretell, prefigure, forecast. In other words, to know what's going to happen!

How to use this word

You could say:

- 'I could not possibly *prognosticate* that I would need an umbrella for the heavy showers – it was sunny when I left.'
- 'I didn't bring the extra money we needed as I assumed we would have enough. *Prognostication* is not one of my talents!'
- 'I can *prognosticate* that Jimmy won't have tidied up for the guests we are expecting, so I'm going home early to do it myself.'

And finally . . .

The last example reminded me of mothers – well, mine anyway! They always seem to know what's going to happen before it does. You are most likely to hear this word in a medical context when, after tests and investigations, you are given a prognosis. (What the doctors expect to happen in the future.) In conversation, this word has the emphasis on the second syllable: **prog-NOST-ik-ate**.

PROPENSITY

I've always used the word tendency, but this means exactly the same thing. I reckon this makes you sound a bit more intelligent, though!

How to use this word

Try writing a letter of complaint in the following way:

'Dear Sir…
When I come into your shop, I have a *propensity* to look at the sale items, but I am often disappointed when I realise that I still can't afford them.'

That should impress them!

On another occasion, you could say:

- 'We don't leave the chocolates out when my mum comes around as she has a *propensity* to eat them all in one go. Instead, we offer her one at a time, thus helping her diet, too.'

And finally . . .

This has the same meaning as the word 'inclination'. The plural, by the way, is 'propensities', should you need it. There's an emphasis on the second syllable when you say this word: **prop-PEN-sitty**.

PUERILE

This is one of the easiest words to describe how to use – it's simply an alternative way to describe someone or something that's childish or juvenile. It comes from the Latin word puerilis ('childish', 'foolish').

How to use this word

You could describe someone's behaviour as 'so *puerile*'.

Better still, during an argument, accuse the other person of having a *puerile* point of view. Or tell that person that the *puerility* of his or her arguments doesn't deserve a response.

And finally . . .

This word is easy to say: **PURE-aisle**. 'Pure' as in orange juice and 'aisle' as in 'lead you up the aisle' to get married. There's a slight emphasis on the first syllable, though.

PUGNACIOUS

This word means quarrelsome, confrontational, belligerent (see page 17), truculent, argumentative, contentious. It comes from the Latin word pugnare ('fight').

How to use this word

You could say, for example:

- 'He was a *pugnacious* man – always squaring up to me.'
- 'Ella's granny was a *pugnacious* old dear, always wanting to fight about something.'
- 'I found him argumentative and *pugnacious*, simply for the sake of it.'
- 'Quite frankly, I found his *pugnacity* irritating.'

And finally . . .

Make sure you put the emphasis on the second syllable when you say this word: **pug-NAY-shush**.

QUINTESSENTIALLY

A word used to describe essentially and characteristically the purest, most typical and perfect form of something.

How to use this word

You could say, for example, that cream teas and cricket on a Sunday afternoon are a *quintessentially* English tradition.

Or maybe Lionel Ritchie love songs are *quintessentially* romantic.

In short, it means 'just a perfect example of...'

And finally . . .

This is used to describe something nice, so you wouldn't normally say 'All the stabbings and shootings in my street are so quintessentially inner city', unless you were being sarcastic, of course! It is pronounced **kwin-tih-SENN-shally**, emphasising the **SENN** part.

REITERATE

This means to say something again or to repeat oneself. It is often used in the spirit of: 'Listen – this is important. Let me say it again so you don't miss the point.'

How to use this word

You might say to your decorator, for example:

- 'Can I just *reiterate* the point that all the borders should be red, and not just upstairs?'

In a letter of complaint to a shop you might write:

- 'After our conversation today, can I *reiterate* the main points with which I am not happy?'

If you're checking a letter for someone or maybe an essay, for example, where there is a lot of repetition, you might say:

- 'There's a lot of *reiteration* in there. Is it all necessary?'

And finally . . .

Make sure you emphasise the **ITT** part of the word when saying it: **ree-ITT-er-ate**.

RIBALD

A great word to use if you want to complain about something you find offensive. It's another word meaning funny, but in a bawdy, racy, naughty, dirty, smutty, lewd, vulgar, gross, coarse, obscene way, often involving jokes, tales or comedy routines about sex.

How to use this word

You could complain:

- 'I found that programme on TV last night too *ribald* and so I will make a complaint about it.'
- 'I don't like your *ribald* language – I find it very offensive.'
- 'The *ribald* nature of that song we heard was unnecessary and I didn't like it one bit, you know.'
- 'He's a *ribald* person, to whom I do not want to listen.'

And finally . . .

This is a word to use when you see/hear something offensive. The 'a' almost becomes a 'u' when you say this word: **RIB-uld**, with the emphasis on the **RIB** part.

RISIBLE

This word means something that relates to laughter – something that's laughable or ludicrous.

How to use this word

You might say:

- 'I looked at my bank statements and saw the *risible* sums of money paid in each month, which my boss described as a salary!'

Risible is not always negative, though – you might say, for example:

- 'I made a list of all the *risible* names of rap stars to try to seem younger and more knowledgeable.'

When complaining, try this approach:

- 'This compensation is *risible* compared with the sum I thought I would get.'

And finally . . .

To recap, imagine using this in place of words such as laughable, silly, funny, etc. It is pronounced **RIZZ-a-bul**, emphasising the **RIZZ**.

RUMBUSTIOUS

This word is used to describe a boisterous, noisy or uproarious crowd; one out of control and unrestrained; an undisciplined crowd and one full of uncontrollable, noisy exuberance (see page 57).

How to use this word

You could say:

- 'The rioting football fans are gathering *rumbustiously* in the town square.'
- 'The fans *rumbustiously* broke down the barriers and invaded the pitch.'
- 'The *rumbustiousness* of the crowd waiting for the start of the January sales was quite overwhelming.'

Perhaps you might want to tell a bunch of noisy children to:

- 'Stop being so *rumbustious*. Calm down and listen to me.'

And finally . . .

When saying this word, the emphasis is on the second syllable, **BUST**. This word is pronounced **rum-BUST-chuss**.

SAGACIOUS

This refers to someone who is shrewd, sharp, quick-witted, erudite, wise, perceptive, astute, learned, far-sighted, all-knowing, intelligent; someone with the ability to make wise judgements; someone who is apt and clever – a perfect description of me! It comes from the Latin word sagax ('wisely').

How to use this word

You could say:

- 'My mum is a *sagacious* person. She told me what to do about this and she was right – again!'
- 'Bridget's *sagacious* choice saved us a lot of time and money in the long run. I'm glad we listened.'
- 'The *sagaciousness* of Diana's decision-making at board level and below still astounds me.'

And finally . . .

This is pronounced **sa-GAY-shuss**, with the emphasis on the **GAY** part of the word.

SALARY/WAGES

Both salary and wages refer to an income for work carried out, whatever its nature. But there's a difference between the two words. Salary refers to a fixed income (for example, a civil servant or lecturer). Wages are received for a more flexible job, perhaps by a student who works varying hours in a shoe shop or by a waitress who works different hours most weeks. It's only a small difference, but knowing the correct facts here may make you look more professional if you are writing to the boss for a rise (by the way, it's only a 'raise' in the USA).

How to use this word

If you are recruiting someone to work for you, then you may want to phrase your monetary offer:

- '*Salary* offered in the region of £40,000 per annum.'

Or

- '*Wages* for the job – £10 per hour.'

Wages are often paid weekly; *salary*, monthly.

And finally . . .

There is always a snobbish element connected to these words. As a general rule, manual workers are paid weekly whereas white-collar workers are paid monthly. So, if you have taken a job as a casual worker but want to convince your new boy or girlfriend that you are a director of the firm for whom you are working, then do not let the word wages slip into your conversation!

SANGUINE

This means optimistic, confident, cheerful, positive, upbeat, hopeful, assured, lively, buoyant.

How to use this word

You might say:

- 'I am less *sanguine* about the prospects of promotion at work, for the competition has been really tough.'
- I am feeling quite *sanguine* about my exam results, which are due out next week.'
- 'I am less *sanguine* about the future than you are. Perhaps I'm more realistic.'

And finally . . .

There's a secondary meaning for this word when used in the correct context. It means 'of the colour red'. In this case you would describe Donald, for example, as having a fresh and sanguine complexion. Make sure you emphasise the first syllable here, pronouncing it **SAN-gwinn**.

SATURNINE

This word means grave, gloomy, dismal, serious and unfriendly, glum, melancholy, sullen, sombre, morose, not talking to anyone, miserable.

How to use this word

You could say:

- 'He gave me such a *saturnine* look that I thought I would go and talk to someone else at the party instead.'

You could also say:

- 'He can be so *saturnine* at times that he's not fun to be with.'
- 'After being dumped by his girlfriend, David walked *saturninely* through the woods to try to clear his mind.'

And finally . . .

Here's what I was thinking when I was writing this: 'I saturninely walked away from the cash point machine empty-handed. I could have sworn there was about five hundred pounds left in there a few days before pay day.' It is pronounced **SAT-er-nine**, with the emphasis on the first syllable.

SATYROMANIAC

This is a little known word used to described a man (never a woman) who is totally and utterly obsessed with, and consumed by, sex. It is the male version of the word nymphomaniac.

How to use this word

Carefully, would be a good start... perhaps among same-sex friends having a laugh and joke.

When you hear a man bragging about his 'romantic conquests', you could accuse him of being a *satyromaniac.*

Women complaining about an unfaithful male partner might accuse him of being a *satyromaniac.*

You might want to tell a 'romantically active man' that his *satyromania* is cool, or unattractive, dangerous, great, happy... or whatever your feelings on the subject happen to be.

And finally . . .

Satyrs were half-men, half-goats – hence 'randy old goat'. When saying this word, it is pronounced **SATTY-ru-main-ee-ac**, emphasising the first part of the word.

SCURRILOUS

This is used to describe strong words that have been said by one person of another person – i.e. someone who makes rude, defamatory, insulting or abusive remarks about someone else.

How to use this word

You could say someone *scurrilously* made his or her point clear.

You could tell someone he or she made the point clear with his or her *scurrilous* words.

You could also say:

- 'He made his views known to everyone at the meeting with his surprisingly *scurrilous* words.'

Alternatively, you could tell someone that you object to his or her *scurrilous* remarks when you hear that person has been saying nasty things about you behind your back.

And finally . . .

This is pretty strong stuff, so save it for the ex-partner or someone as equally distasteful! It is pronounced **SCURRY-luss**, with a slight emphasis on the first part.

SIC

A fascinating word because it is one of the few words in the English language that's only ever written and never spoken! It literally means: 'And I was quoting there, they're not my words.'

How to use this word

For example, if you were writing to your boss asking for a rise, you might say: 'And furthermore, Robin the supervisor says I am a hard-working, reliable, dedicated member of the team (*sic*).' In other words, the supervisor has used those words.

You can also use it to separate yourself from someone you are quoting who uses incorrect grammar, or who gets a geographical or historical fact wrong. For example:

- 'My friend says: "We should go to Madrid, the capital of France, this summer" (*sic*).'

In other words, your friend is the one lacking intelligence, not you!

When complaining, you may wish to say:

- 'The cashier said she was sick and tired of dealing with miserable, moaning, old clients such as me (*sic*).'

In other words, I don't see myself in that way!

SIMILE

This is a figure of speech that compares things and that generally contains the words 'like' or 'as'. For example: 'As high as a kite' or 'As daft as a brush.'

Other similes include:

- As bold as brass.
- As bright as a button.
- As dry as a bone.
- As quick as a flash.
- Working like a dog.

A simile should not be confused with a metaphor which is a colourful description of something that's not quite literal.

For example:

- He showered her with gifts
- You are the sunshine of my life
- He is a giant in his field of expertise

And finally . . .

The use of the word 'as' is usually a good clue that something is a simile. Emphasise the **SIM** part of the word: **SIM-il-lee**.

STENTORIAN

This word is used to describe someone who has a very loud and powerful voice – simple as that! Such a person would be described as having a stentorian voice. In street slang, 'someone with a big gob'! The word comes from Stentor, a very loud man in the Trojan army. This Greek herald was supposed to have the voice of fifty men.

How to use this word

You could say, for example:

- 'The Sergeant-Major always gave his command in that well-known *stentorian* voice of his.'

You could complain that a store manager seemed to have a *stentorian* voice when expressing his views, which was most unacceptable.

It is also correct to say that, when the adverts come on TV, you've noticed they're at a *stentorian* volume.

And finally . . .

When saying this word, it is pronounced **sten-TORE-ian**, with the middle syllable sounding the loudest.

STERTOROUS

This word is used to describe hoarse, laboured, gasping, harsh and noisy breathing or snoring. There aren't many words to describe snoring, so remember this one! It can also be used to describe the heavy breathing of someone wide awake. It comes from the Latin word stertere ('snore').

How to use this word

You could complain that someone's *stertorous* snoring kept you awake all night, or that this person *stertorously* kept you awake.

You could also say:

- 'I could hear some *stertorous* breathing as I was giving my presentation. Was someone asleep?'
- 'Andrew *stertorously* made his presence known' (i.e. because he's a naturally noisy breather by habit, or maybe he just fell asleep and snored!).

And finally . . .

Make sure the emphasis is on the first syllable when you say this word: **STERT-ur-uss**.

STOIC

This word means void, unaffected or indifferent to feeling or emotion. A stoic is often the description given to someone who endures a painful illness without complaint.

How to use this word

You could refer to a sales assistant, for example, as *stoically* listening to your complaint.

Other ways to use this word might be:

- 'My girlfriend has suddenly ended our two-year relationship, but I didn't let her see that it bothered me. I just sat there and listened to her reasons and, when she had finished, I *stoically* stood up, smiled and left.'
- 'Kieran has *stoically* endured years of pain' (i.e. without complaint).

And finally . . .

You can always describe someone as having a stoic response. It sounds so much better than saying someone didn't give a damn! It is pronounced **STOW-ik**, emphasising the first syllable. **STOW** rhymes with 'low' (as in 'low down').

SUPERCILIOUS

This refers to someone who is disdainfully arrogant, pompous, patronising, superior, condescending and disdainful; someone who acts as if other people's opinions don't matter in any way and who considers them, as a whole, to be inferior to his or her own opinions.

How to use this word

You could say:

- 'The girl had a *supercilious* expression. She seemed to be looking down her nose at the camera, as if she was better than the rest of us.'
- 'He spoke to me in a rather sickeningly *supercilious* voice, which made me feel useless.'
- 'The manager dealt with my complaint in a very *supercilious* manner.'

And finally . . .

I would explain further, but you don't need to know it, really, and if I did take the time you probably wouldn't understand it anyway so, before you slam the book down in a temper, that's me being supercilious! When saying this word, it is pronounced **super-SIL-ius**, with the **SIL** part sounding the loudest.

SUPERFLUOUS

This means excessive, surplus, extra, needless, unnecessary, not essential. In other words, much more than what is needed. It comes from the Latin word supervacuus ('unnecessary', 'extra').

How to use this word

You might say:

- 'I was trying to build the wardrobe, but there was a mass of *superfluous* detail in the instructions, which made it very confusing.'
- 'Why is there always a *superfluous* amount of jelly at every child's party we organise? It usually all ends up on the floor, anyway.'

I'd like to say, if only it were true:

- 'Often, when I check my bank account, I find there's thousands of pounds left over every month, *superfluous* to my needs.'

(Well, just dreaming!)

And finally . . .

I was going to add another twenty-five examples here but I felt that would be superfluous to your needs. Put the emphasis on the **PER** part of this word when saying it: **soo-PER-flew-uss**.

SURREPTITIOUS

This is sly, hidden, secret, underhand by stealth; sneaky, clandestine, furtive. The opposite of all these words is 'open'. In other words, it describes someone doing something sneakily so that nobody else notices. It comes from the Latin word surripere ('to take away secretly').

How to use this word

You could say:

- 'I'm sorry that I keep looking *surreptitiously* at my watch. It's just that my train leaves in five minutes.'
- 'Kizzy was *surreptitiously* turning the newspaper upside down to peek at the crossword answers.'
- 'I have noticed your *surreptitious* glances at the recipe book, mother. I would have thought you would know how to bake a cake by now!'

And finally . . .

This is pronounced **surrup-TISH-uss**, with the emphasis on the **TISH** part.

SYCOPHANT

This word is used to describe someone who flatters and praises a powerful person for his or her own personal gain. In other words, a creep! A sycophant is slavish, toady, a groveller, flatterer and fawner.

How to use this word

You might want to use this word to describe that creep at work who likes to suck up to the boss! He is the 'yes man' we all despise so much: the one who always agrees with the boss, constantly telling him or her how great his or her ideas are.

You could say:

- 'He's a *sycophant.* He's only working overtime to get into the boss's good books.'

You can also accuse the office creep of making *sycophantic* remarks.

And finally . . .

This is pronounced **SIC-o-fant**, with the emphasis on the first syllable (**SIC**), which in turn rhymes with 'lick'.

SYNERGY

This describes two things that work together to achieve, as a partnership, more than they would individually. It's the combined effort of the two things that power each thing.

How to use this word

You could say:

- 'We need to be helping each other to get results. There's a lack of *synergy* in the sales team.'
- 'Newspaper and radio advertising work in *synergy* to get the clients' products out to the public.'
- 'David is mowing the back lawn and Elizabeth is mowing the front lawn. They're working successfully in *synergy*.'

And finally . . .

When writing this book, my imagination and hands have worked together in perfect synergy, thinking of the big words and then typing them up! This word is pronounced **SIN-er-jee**, emphasising the first syllable.

SYNONYMOUS

This literally means that something is the same, or almost the same, as something else, or that one thing can be closely identified with another.

How to use this word

You could say that clothing brand X is *synonymous* with great style.

You could also say:

- 'Celebrity chef A is *synonymous* with great-tasting food.'
- 'Saddam Hussein's regime was *synonymous* with fear.'

And finally . . .

In other words, this can be used to link two things together through similarity. It is pronounced **sin-NON-a-muss**, heavy on the **NON** part.

TACITURN

This word means reserved, silent, quiet, aloof, cold, distant, saying very little. It also means reticent, introverted, uncommunicative, tight-lipped. It comes from the Latin word tacitus ('silent').

How to use this word

You might say:

- 'Charlotte is a little *taciturn*. She doesn't say much, but seems to be listening to everyone.'
- 'I might be slightly *taciturn* by nature, but I'm taking it all in and mentally jotting it down.'
- 'Emma comes across as quite *taciturn* by nature, but she warms up as she gets to know you.'

Perhaps in a different context:

- 'He's a miserable, *taciturn*, rude little man.'

And finally . . .

Basically, this just describes someone who's quiet. Whether you use it in a mean way or an observational way is down to how you say it and in what context. It is pronounced **TASS-i-turn**, with the **TASS** part being emphasised.

TANGIBLE

This means something that's physical, real, actual, solid, concrete, material, evident, plain, touchable. Or something that's real to a person, like a perk in a job. Companies talk about their tangible assets – the property and equipment they own – as opposed to the firm's value through market share or goodwill, etc. It refers to things you can actually touch. It comes from the Latin word tangere ('touch').

How to use this word

You might say:

- 'One of the *tangible* benefits of joining the health club is getting your own locker.'
- 'The police need *tangible* evidence before they can charge this man.'
- 'I haven't stolen anything. What *tangible* evidence do you have to support your claim?'

And finally . . .

The 'g' in tangible is soft, sounding like the letter 'j' (in the same way both the 'g's in George are soft). This is pronounced **TANJ-ib-ul**, with the first syllable being emphasised.

TEMPORISE

This means to delay making a decision, to stall, to procrastinate (see page 146), to fence, to play for time, avoiding commitment, hesitating to gain advantage, evasively prolonging a discussion. It's a word often used when discussing serious issues like contracts. Not an everyday word, but it is good to know the facts, as it will pop up in situations involving business and the law.

How to use this word

You could say:

- 'I feel the purchasers of my house may be *temporising* to see if I will lower my asking price.'
- 'Paula has the contracts for the new deal we're working on, but the other side has *temporised* to see if we panic.'
- 'The two sides have both prolonged their negotiations to try to reach a better settlement. *Temporising* seems to have generated more discussion.'

And finally . . .

In the USA, this is spelt 'temporize'. Make sure you emphasise the first syllable here: **TEMP-or-eyes**.

TENEBROUS

This means dark, gloomy, shady, unlit, murky, shut off from the light, shadowy. It's not a very well-known word, but it is worth trotting out to use in a sentence now and again.

How to use this word

You could use it to describe a room. For example:

- 'It's a bit *tenebrous* and unwelcoming, isn't it? I think £80 a week rent is too much.'

Or

- 'Let's paint the office white, pull the blinds back and make it brighter and less *tenebrous*.'

You could also say:

- 'The boys walked down the scary, *tenebrous* alley late at night in search of the… kebab van!'

And finally . . .

This is a cool, simple, descriptive word that doesn't seem to be used much, so here's your chance to use it – perhaps to complain about something. It is pronounced **TEN-e-brus**, emphasising the first syllable.

TITIVATING

This means to smarten up, put finishing touches to, spruce up, tart up, dress up, adorn, beautify, do up. An excellent example is someone putting the final touches to his or her look: adjusting their tie or hair is the act of titivating.

How to use this word

You could say to someone who is constantly adjusting his or her clothing and general appearance:

- 'Stop *titivating* yourself – you look fantastic as you are.'

You could also say:

- 'Aisha is upstairs *titivating* before the guests arrive.'
- 'After hours of *titivation*, you still look lovely, dear.'
- 'She's such a *titivator*, a real perfectionist, but she always looks good as a result.'

And finally . . .

This is pronounced **TITTA-vate-ing**, emphasising the first part of the word.

TOOTHSOME

Here's a great word that you don't hear very often, and it's got nothing at all to do with teeth! It literally describes something that tastes nice, or is sexually attractive.

How to use this word

You could describe some food as absolutely *toothsome*, or say that it could hardly be described as *toothsome*.

Alternatively, you could describe a new, young model as a *toothsome* young woman with star quality!

Just as you might refer to a business deal as a sexy proposition, you could also describe it as *toothsome*. So a man, woman or an opportunity could be either sexy or *toothsome*.

And finally . . .

So go on, add a little colour to your language by describing someone or something as toothsome. Maybe not the dentist, as this may become confusing! This is pronounced **TOOTH-sum**, emphasising the first half of the word.

TORPID

This word is used to describe someone who is a bit slow, sluggish, apathetic, dormant, lacking in energy; someone with no vigour and who is almost dormant! It's sometimes used to describe an animal coming out of hibernation.

How to use this word

You could describe your partner in the morning as *torpid*, and that would be just one word to describe him or her instead of all the above.

Maybe you'd like to complain about a shop assistant who was slow and couldn't be bothered to serve you. You could describe this assistant as *torpid*.

And finally . . .

Of course, whether you use this as a good-natured, funny description or as a nasty, stinging remark is, like so many words, all in how you say it. There's lots of ways to use this word, and it just rolls of the tongue nicely like a verbal weapon! This is pronounced **TOR-pid**, with the emphasis on the first half.

TRANSITORY

This word means brief, temporary, passing, fleeting, short-lived, momentary, of brief duration, transient. In other words, something that doesn't last very long. It comes from the Latin word transitus ('crosing, passing over').

How to use this word

You could say:

- 'That fashion was popular but *transitory*: it was only around for a few months.'

When complaining, maybe you could say:

- 'My wardrobe is full of *transitory* fashions – nothing looks good anymore.'

You could also say:

- 'We'll make a *transitory* visit to your office later to discuss the matter further.'

And finally . . .

My New Year's resolution to give up smoking every 1st January always turns out to be transitory! Make sure you emphasise the first syllable here: **TRANS-it-tree**.

TRANSLUCENT

This refers to light passing through something that is not quite transparent, so that the effect is a glow. Objects on the other side can be made out slightly, but cannot be clearly distinguished. Tracing paper is translucent. The frosted glass fitted into bathroom windows is translucent. It comes from the Latin word luceo ('shine').

How to use this word

You could say:

- 'The *translucency* of this glass means that nobody can see me when I am in the bathroom.'
- 'This plastic vase is pretty and light, and the *translucent* design is very attractive.'
- 'The clouds that thinly stretch across the sky today are sufficiently *translucent* to show the moon, which has just appeared.'

Or

- 'The clouds' *translucence* allows me to see the moon.'

And finally . . .

When saying this word, it is pronounced **trans-LOOS-sunt**, with the emphasis on the second syllable (**LOOS**, not LOOZ).

TREFOIL

A trefoil is a shape or design similar to a three-leaved clover. An example of this is the CND sign. If a design is three lobed, then it's described as trefoil. It comes from the Latin word trifolium ('three leaved').

How to use this word

There are no complicated ways to use this word. It's just a case of recognising a design with three, relatively equally spaced, pointed bits!

So you could say:

- 'That's a wonderful *trefoil* design.'
- 'Can we have the design without the *trefoils* included?'
- 'Maybe the *trefoils* on that design should be more detailed.'

And finally . . .

This is a word that is used in art and design, and it is one that is sometimes used to describe other things, too, perhaps by a decorator or dress designer. In horticulture, a trifoliate leaf is divided into three. In short, it's a handy word to know, just in case! It is pronounced **tre-FOIL**, emphasising the **FOIL** (not TREE-FOIL).

TREPIDATION

This refers to a state of alarm, dread, fear, apprehension or to a severe nervousness of the mind. It is used when talking about a concern or anxiety for a forthcoming event. It comes from the Latin word trepidus ('flurried').

How to use this word

You could say:

- 'Rachael proceeded with *trepidation* when it came to climbing the mountain, because it was so high and she was scared.'
- 'When I think about those exams coming up, despite all the revision I've done, I feel a certain amount of *trepidation*.'
- 'I may use your shop again, but with a certain amount of *trepidation* – indeed, if at all – unless you sort out this problem.'

And finally . . .

This is pronounced **treppa-DAY-shun**, heavy on the **DAY** part of the word.

TRISKAIDEKAPHOBIA

This is a great word, but it takes ages to learn to spell it! It means 'a phobia/morbid fear of the number 13'. It's not a word used every day but it's useful to know nevertheless, and it might well come up in a pub quiz. Every Friday the 13th at work when there's some sort of discussion about the unlucky date – that will be your chance to use this word. But you'll need to practise saying it first. So stand in front of the mirror, looking confident, raise your eyebrows and let it roll off the tongue! It comes from the Greek word treiskaideka ('thirteen').

How to use this word

You could say:

- 'So, you suffer from *triskaidekaphobia*, then?'
- 'I suffer from *triskaidekaphobia*.'
- 'I am *triskaidekaphobic*.'
- 'Are you *triskaidekaphobic*?'
- 'I went into work today on Friday the 13th, despite being severely *triskaidekaphobic*.'

And finally . . .

This is pronounced (after a lot of practice) **trisk-eye-DEKKA-fow-beer**.

UBIQUITOUS

This means something that is everywhere at the same time, in many places simultaneously. I suppose it could be used to describe most working parents! It comes from the Latin word ubique ('everywhere').

How to use this word

You could say:

- 'I've had enough of these new *ubiquitous* i-pods. Everyone's walking about nodding their heads to music and looking ridiculous.'

- 'Short skirts seem to be in fashion this year, along with the *ubiquitous* white socks, of course.'

- 'Television, the most *ubiquitous* of household entertainment products, is entering a new age, with Freeview, satellite and cable becoming readily available to a new generation.'

And finally . . .

Surely, aren't all mothers ubiquitous? There's no getting away from them. However busy they are, they are always there to help and guide – and they're always right, too! Make sure you emphasise the **BICK** part of this word when saying it: **you-BICK-wit-uss**.

UNIMPEACHABLE

This means flawless, faultless, blameless, impeccable, impossible to discredit, perfect. It's used to describe a person of such a high moral stand that there is no way he or she can be criticised, doubted or dishonoured in any way; a word attributed to someone who's so faultless he or she is beyond reproach.

How to use this word

You might describe your boss as a person of *unimpeachable* integrity.

You could describe a witness to a crime as *unimpeachable*.

You could also say:

- 'The journalist described the man from the White House as an *unimpeachable* source of gossip, having worked there for so long.'

And finally . . .

When saying this word, you pronounce it **un-im-PEECH-ab-ul**, with the emphasis on the third syllable.

UNPERTURBED

This word means calm, tranquil, composed, cool, at ease, placid, untroubled. It also means unruffled and serene.

How to use this word

You could say:

- 'All hell broke loose at work when all the computers went down at once, but I remained *unperturbed* and called the IT emergency hotline while everyone else was screaming!'
- 'I was totally *unperturbed* by all the waiters in your restaurant shouting and running around, but my 102-year-old mother was a bit confused.'

And finally . . .

Just imagine you are saying 'I was laid back and cool about it all', stick in the word unperturbed and you'll get it right! The correct pronunciation of the word is **unpa-TERBD**, with the emphasis on the second half of the word.

VAPID

This refers to someone or something that is dull, lifeless, spiritless, flat, without interest. It comes from the Latin word vapidus ('spiritless').

How to use this word

You could say:

- 'I'm not enjoying this book. The storyline seems to be rather *vapid*.'
- 'The architecture of this period seems *vapid* in comparison with the Victorian era.'

Maybe when complaining to a shop you could say:

- 'Since your new floor layout and products, I have found your range *vapid* compared with your old selection.'

You could also say:

- 'The *vapidity* of this novel (or show or trip, etc.) is driving me crazy.'

And finally . . .

Make sure you emphasise the first syllable here when using this in conversation: **VAY-pid**.

VERACIOUS

This means to speak with truth, accuracy and honesty; to be precise and frank in your words. It comes from the Latin word verax ('true').

How to use this word

You could say:

- 'Carol speaks with such *veracity*, there's no need to doubt her for a second.'
- 'His *veracious* comments come straight from the heart: I believe everything he has to say.'
- 'It's a shame that I never feel politicians speak with much *veracity*, because it means I am never sure whether to believe their policies or not.'

And finally . . .

The emphasis is on the second syllable here: **ver-AY-shuss**.

VERBATIM

This means to repeat exactly in writing or when speaking the words written or spoken by someone else; a direct copy or quotation; a written, word-by-word account or an exact repeat of dialogue. It comes from the Latin word verbum ('word').

How to use this word

You may want to say:

- 'I can't repeat the conversation I had with the manager *verbatim*, but basically I was told x, y and z.'

You may want to ask someone who wants you to read something to him or her whether he or she wants the gist of it, the main message, or whether he or she would like you to read it *verbatim* – word for word.

Alternatively, you could say you relayed the latest piece of gossip you overheard in the works canteen, *verbatim*!

And finally . . .

This is pronounced **ver-BAY-tum**. It's rather like a written or vocal photocopier.

VERNACULAR

This word refers to a person's speech; to his or her local informal accent, colloquial tongue, native and indigenous style; to a person's dialect and lingo. It comes from the Latin word vernaculus ('native').

How to use this word

You could say:

- 'Her interesting Cornish *vernacular* is part of her personality.'
- 'The Polish students found it hard to understand Glaswegian *vernacular* when they arrived at the college.'
- 'The millionaire businessman is proud of his strong East End *vernacular* because it reminds him of his impoverished roots.'

And finally . . .

If you use this word instead of the phrase, 'local accent', then you will be correct. It is pronounced **ver-NAK-you-la**, with the emphasis on the **NAK** part of the word.

VEXILLOLOGY

Vexillology is the study of flags (and their history), emblems, maritime badges and symbols. It is also linked to the study of heraldry. The vexillum was a flag/banner used in the Roman Empire. It comes, therefore, from the Latin word vexillum ('flag', 'banner').

How to use this word

Next time you talk to someone about flags you could say:

- 'There's a huge selection of *vexillum* items for sale in this shop.'

You could also say:

- 'I like *vexillology*, learning about flags, symbols and historical badges, although my *vexillological* knowledge is still very basic.'

- 'My friend should be a *vexillologist* because he can recognise the national flags of so many countries.'

And finally . . .

To study, design, make or advise in some of these fields would make you a vexillologist. This word is pronounced **vex-il-OLL-ij-ee**.

VOLTE-FACE

This describes a sudden change of mind, an about turn of something, a change of heart or a turn to the opposite direction.

How to use this word

You could say, for example:

- 'In the light of the unions threatening a month-long walkout, in a sudden *volte-face* the company announced a pay rise.'
- 'The government's performed a *volte-face* on its policy on Iraq and decided to pull out all its troops.'

And finally . . .

In everyday life, if someone with whom you are dealing changes his or her position in a disagreement or a situation, then you can describe this as a volte-face (a change of heart). This word is pronounced **VOLT-FASS**, with equal emphasis on both syllables.

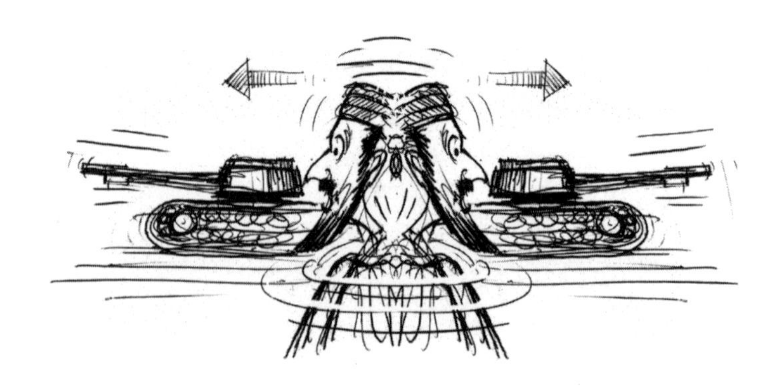

XENOPHOBIA

Hurray, I've found a word beginning with the letter X! Xenophobia refers to a morbid dislike or fear of strangers and their customs. It comes from the Greek word xenos ('stranger').

How to use this word

You could refer to someone as being *xenophobic* because he or she refuses to be nice to visiting tourists or to the immigrants moving in next door. Or you could simply accuse that person of being *xenophobic* in his or her attitudes or actions.

Alternatively, you could say to him or her:

- 'You are a *xenophobe*!'

To which he or she might reply:

- 'I have a *xenophobic* dislike of anything that's not English.'

And finally . . .

Xenophobia is actually pronounced **zenna-FOBE-ear**, emphasising the **FOBE**.

ZEALOUS

I had to have a word beginning with the letter Z! If I didn't put in zealous, which can be used in conversation, then I'd have to put in zebu, which is the humped ox of Asia. Can't really see that being very useful when writing a letter of complaint to a restaurant, can you? Unless, of course, the humped ox of Asia was sitting on your table – unlikely – so zealous it is then! It means eager, keen, passionate, enthusiastic, fanatical, obsessive, devoted, keen.

How to use this word

You could say:

- 'I am a *zealous* supporter of the Liberal Democrat Party.'

Or

- 'I show a great *zeal* for the Liberal Democrat Party.'
- 'I *zealously* follow the Liberal Democrat campaign trail.'

And finally . . .

When you say this word, it's pronounced **ZELL-uss**, emphasising the first syllable.

PENULTIMATE

This word actually means the last but one, the second to last or the one before the last. You'll note that this word has slipped out of alphabetical order and is actually the one before the last in the book! Penultimate comes from the Latin words paene ('almost') and ultimus ('last').

How to use this word

You might say:

- 'This is the *penultimate* week of school before they break up for the summer holidays.'
- 'This book is the *penultimate* in the series, but make sure you read them in order or you'll lose the plot.'

And finally . . .

Just imagine you're swapping the term 'one before the last' with the word penultimate and you will be correct. The 'one before the one before the last one' has the even more snappy title 'ante-penultimate'. So 23 December is the ante penultimate day before Christmas Day! Meanwhile the word *penultimate* is pronounced **pen-ULT-im-ate**, with the stress on the second part.

DEFINITIVE

This means final, not able to be improved, complete, conclusive. This is the final word in the book – it's not just thrown together, you know!

How to use this word

If you're playing in a quiz, you can ask someone if that's his or her *definitive* answer.

You could also say:

- 'There is no *definitive* proof that UFOs exist.'
- 'There are no *definitive* answers to this problem – we just don't know.'
- 'The police had no *definitive* proof that Fred stole the money, so they had to let him go.'

And finally . . .

That is my definitive guide to using big words! When saying this word, it is pronounced **dif-FIN-it-iv**, emphasising the second syllable **FIN**.

AND TO CONCLUDE, SOME WEIRD LONG WORDS – JUST FOR FUN!

LLANFAIRPWLLGWYNGYLLGOGERYCH-WYRNDROBWLLLLANTYSILIO-GOGOGOCH

A village in North Wales.

FLOCCINAUCINIHILIPILIFICATION

This means to reduce to nothing, or the estimation of something as worth nothing.

ANTIDISESTABLISHMENTARIANISM

A word meaning someone who is against those who are opposed to having a church that is connected to and supported by the state.

HEPATICOCHOLANGIOCHOLECYSTEN-TEROSTOMIES

This is the word for an operation involving the gall bladder.

But the grand winner is the (all one word) 1,913-letter chemical name for tryptophan synthetase (a protein). There does, however, seem to be a few variations on this word, with a number of letters added or taken away!

**methionylglutaminylarginyltyrosylglu-
tamylserylleucylphenylalanylalanylgluta-
minylleucyllysylglutamylarginyllysylglu-
tamylglycylalanylphenylalanylvalylpro-
lylphenylalanylvalylthreonylleucylglycylas-
partylprolylglycylisoleucylglutamylgluta-
minylserylleucyllysylisoleucylaspartylthre-
onylleucylisoleucylglutamylalanylglycy-
lalanylaspartylalanylleucylglutamylleucyl-
glycylisoleucylprolylphenylalanylserylas-
partylprolylleucylalanylaspartylglycylpro-
lylthreonylisoleucylglutaminylasparaginy-
lalanylthreonylleucylarginylalanylpheny-
lalanylalanylalanylglycylvalylthreonylpro-
lylalanylglutaminylcysteinylphenylalanyl-
glutamylmethionylleucy-
lalanylleucylisoleucylarginylglutaminylly-
sylhistidylprolylthreonylisoleucylpro-
lylisoleucylglycylleucylleucylmethionylty-
rosylalanylasparaginylleucylvalylpheny-
lalanylasparaginyllysylglycylisoleucylas-
partylglutamylphenylalanyltyrosylalanyl-
glutaminylcysteinylglutamyllysylvalylgly-
cylvalylaspartylserylvalylleucylvalylalany-
laspartylvalylprolylvalylglutaminylglu-
tamylserylalanylprolylphenylalanylarginyl-
glutaminylalanylalanylleucylarginylhistidy-
lasparaginylvalylalanylpro-**

lylisoleucylphenylalanylisoleucylcysteinyl-
prolylprolylaspartylalanylaspartylasparty-
laspartylleucylleucylarginylgluta-
minylisoleucylalanylseryltyrosylglycy-
larginylglycyltyrosylthreonyltyro-
sylleucylleucylserylarginylalanylglycylva-
lylthreonylglycylalanylglutamylas-
paraginylarginylalanylalanylleucylpro-
lylleucylasparaginylhistidylleucylvaly-
lalanyllysylleucyllysylglutamyltyrosylas-
paraginylalanylalanylprolylprolylleucylglut-
aminylglycylphenylalanylgly-
cylisoleucylserylalanylprolylaspartylgluta-
minylvalyllysylalanylalanylisoleucylas-
partylalanylglycylalanylalanylglycy-
lalanylisoleucylserylglycylsery-
lalanylisoleucylvalyllysylisoleucylisoleucyl-
glutamylglutaminylhistidylas-
paraginylisoleucylglutamylprolylglu-
tamyllysylmethionylleucylalany-
lalanylleucyllysylvalylphenylalanylvalylglu-
taminylprolylmethionyllysylalany-
lalanylthreonylarginylserine